Creative
COTTAGE CRAFT

COMPILED BY STEPHANIE SIMES

A J.B. Fairfax Press Publication

CONTENTS

FOREWORD

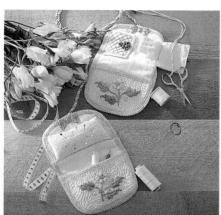

From Mumruffin Cottage, her home cum studio in the beautiful
countryside outside Sydney, Stephanie has gathered this
delightful collection of country crafts.

Following her simple instructions, you can bring all the charm of
a country cottage into your own home with these delightful quilts,
cushions, pictures and more.

EDITORIAL
Managing Editor: Judy Poulos
Editorial Assistant: Ella Martin
Editorial Coordinator: Margaret Kelly
Photography: Andrew Elton
Styling: Kathy Tripp
Illustrations: Lesley Griffith

DESIGN AND PRODUCTION
Manager: Anna Maguire
Design: Jenny Nossal
Photo Editor: Stacey Strickland

Layout: Sheridan Packer
Cover Design: Jenny Pace

Published by J.B. Fairfax Press Pty Limited
80-82 McLachlan Ave, Rushcutters Bay 2011
Australia
A.C.N. 003 738 430

Formatted by J.B. Fairfax Press Pty Limited

Printed by Toppan Printing Company,
Singapore

JBFP 447

COTTAGE CRAFTS
ISBN 1 86343 279 5

INTRODUCTION

In some parts of the craft world, precision is often the order of the day and can be quite daunting. In this book, I wanted to create some projects to challenge the experienced and stimulate the beginner, yet ensure that all the projects are achievable.

You may wish to use different colours and, especially with the wool embroidery, different wools, if necessary. Those listed are meant to be used as a guide. If you don't have all the requirements, but you have a basketful of wools, improvise.

Don't unpick, unless you are really unhappy with your work. Stitching should be enjoyable and, in this rushed world of ours, those stolen moments should be treasured. Looking at your finished project up on the wall is the reward, not examining the back of your project for its tidiness. The back of all my work is extremely messy. The only rule I have is that from the front of your work you should not be able to see the threads you have carried across the back. This applies mainly to crewel embroidery, as the beauty of wool is that it can be covered with fabric.

I hope you enjoy all these projects, many of which have been taught at Mumruffin Cottage. Thank you for all those who participated in the classes and helped construct these projects. Thanks to those participants who created and taught their wonderful projects, Carol Kinross, Brooke Rozorio, Annette Phelps, Helen Redenbach, Jane Toohey and to Helen Greenacre whose profiles give an insight into the souls of these characters.

I would also like to thank the following people: Jenny Taylor, for her precision lifesaving stitching; Lisa Johnson, for her continual guidance and advice; my sister-in-law, Winsome Watts and my sister, Danielle McDonald, for their advice, help and encouragement; my parents, Jann and Murray Watts who have always inspired me to create and to enjoy nature; the members of the Nowra sewing group who are a great source of encouragement and inspiration for all sewers and a wonderful support for each other; my family, Lee, Monty, Dorian and Millie, for their patience and encouragement and to whom I dedicate this book; Judy Poulos and J.B. Fairfax Press, for taking a risk on this project and giving Mumruffin Cottage a chance. Judy has the amazing ability to change a complicated instruction into an easy direction, with the patience of a saint; and especially to all sewers – you can do whatever you want with whatever medium you wish to use – experiment.

Don't be restricted by 'the rules'. Some rules really
are meant to be broken!

Stephanie

PROFILES

By Helen Greenacre

STEPHANIE SIMES

The genesis of this book arises from a combination of Stephanie's energy to create, her belief that with a little courage other women can be engaged in satisfying and challenging projects with a needle and thread, and her desire to gather and share the talent in the Shoalhaven.

Coming from an energetic family, Stephanie is never idle. Her childhood was spent on a dairy farm at Pyree, which combined a freedom of spirit, a love of nature, and the inspiration of a creative energetic mother who was involved in art, home decorating, gardening and teaching children. Stephanie relishes a quick completion, practical reward, and believes that, as with gardening, you never unpick what you can cover with a forget-me-not.

A friend's attention to the lace insertion of her wedding dress led her to learn lace insertion and to do Jane Toohey's embroidery and smocking courses. The satisfaction she gained from these crafts encouraged her to experiment with design and unconventional mediums.

The link between sewing and nurturing is an elemental one; as Stephanie says, she can breastfeed and smock at the same time. Craft and sewing offer a quantifiable result for which mothers of young children often feel a need.

Stephanie's husband built her a timber cottage on their property – Mumruffin Cottage – and from this cosy workshop, where women come for fellowship and inspiration, she began to share her talents and those of the teachers she gathered.

This book is the extension of the success of Mumruffin Cottage, with Stephanie wishing to share the talents of the teachers of the area with a wider community.

CAROL ANN KINROSS

Carol became interested in patchwork on a very basic level when pregnant with her first child. Using the scraps from the bassinet and cot blankets she had made, 'A trip around the world' quilt was born.

Four children and working full-time left little opportunity to pursue her growing interest, but when the family was relocated to the United States in 1985, she quickly signed up for a class at a local store. Carol's teacher, the store owner, asked Carol to replace her in teaching the patchwork classes.

Over the next four years, with her family's support, she spent many happy hours teaching classes in patchwork, quilting and stencilling. Aside from the pleasure of seeing colours merge and patterns come alive with the enthusiasm of students, Carol gained the friendship – some lifelong, some fleeting – of the many people of all ages and walks of life who passed through the classes over the years.

Since returning home, she has begun teaching again, which is a constant source of delight, challenge, companionship, and a voyage of learning that she will always treasure.

JANE TOOHEY

As Jane looks from her pine worktable towards the cattle in lush kikuyu pasture, the hills around Berry remind her of her childhood landscape around the family farm at Hawks Bay, New Zealand.

Jane was inspired in design and painting by her art teacher at boarding school and later, her artistic inclination came through when she managed Suomi, a shop in Sydney which traded in Marrimekko, glass and fabric of Finnish and Italian design. Together with Greg Toohey, then a sari-draped poet and musician, she moved in a hippie, 'muso' group.

After her triplets were born, Jane began to sew and sketch. Her smocking and garden stitchery were originally inspired by her mother. She began with drawn-thread work, cross stitch and calico skirts with flowers bunching from the pockets. Jane developed her own unique style with the help of a small booklet, *A Hundred Stitches*, and an active imagination, an artistic flare and her ability to improvise and teach stitches which were new to embroiderers.

When the family moved to Berry, NSW, Jane and Greg held annual 'Exquisitions', gathering their own art and that of other local artists. Jane painted wood-turned skittles, door wedges, light pulls and skipping ropes, wooden beds and trunks.

Jane does wool embroidery, smocking, lacework, and she invents patterns and scenes and inhabits them with fanciful folk. She teaches and continually develops her talents with a unique flare and a style which reflects her personal charm and serenity.

BROOKE ROZORIO

Brooke remembers being dressed in overalls, made from her grandfather's old fine-wool suits, with ducks lovingly embroidered by her grandmother on the bib. Her grandmother taught her to sew during the holidays spent with her in Dubbo.

When Brooke moved from the city to the weatherboard post office in Terara, she was inspired to furnish the 1871 dwelling in a style respectful of its age and history. With a fascination for fabric-damask and tapestry and with her talent in crafts, Brooke has created the atmosphere of a comfortable home. Recently, she returned to Dubbo and, visiting her grandmother's house, recognised how it echoed the home she has created for her family. Stitchery weaves a thread throughout four generations of Brooke's family.

At present Brooke is doing an Associated Diploma in Teacher Librarianship. 'At the end of each submission I sew for days' she says.

She is part of a sewing circle that meets weekly. This link with a close, supportive and convivial group of sewers has made her move to the country easier.

ANNETTE PHELPS

Annette had a fantasy to become a sculptor and work in clay. However, she married into the florist business and, as she learnt the trade, she discovered a talent and interest that she could express with flowers. She has managed her own studio for the past ten years. 'Every day I learn something new' she says.

Annette, who was always interested in design, interiors and has a passion for colour, trained with TAFE for four years – three in Commercial Floristry at Wollongong, then a year in Advanced Floristry at Sydney TAFE. She still attends many workshops and seminars from which she draws new ideas.

With flare, Annette combines her knowledge and instinct of texture and colour, using monochromatic themes in designs. Gardens and the countryside, whether wheat stacks or seasonal crops, provide inspiration.

She conducts private classes as well as those for Shoalhaven Adult Education. With growing confidence, Annette perceives more possibilities for her energies and is open to more ideas to incorporate in her art work.

An impulsive creator, she says 'It is nothing for me to repaint a room at home on a sudden impulse, and my husband wonders if he has walked into the right house.'

HELEN REDENBACH

Born in Nowra, Helen has lived in the Shoalhaven all of her life and cannot remember a time when she hasn't sewn. Whether for brides or debutantes, idealists or amateur sewers, she is able to piece together the dreams of her clients from the photos, video clippings or the fabric scraps they bring along. Creative and versatile, she adjusts to the hazards of satin or the unpredictable angles of crazy patchwork.

Her parents encouraged self-reliance. By the time she left school, her mother had taught her to make her own clothes on their old Singer treadle machine, and as her mother was a perfectionist, Helen did a lot of unpicking.

Helen, with help from her mother, made her own wedding gown, bridesmaids' gowns and mother-of-the-bride outfit. Her mother also made and decorated the wedding cake.

When her four children were small, Helen not only made all their clothes, but remembers also making stuffed toys, robots and dinosaurs.

She now runs a thriving seamstress business from home, and particularly enjoys heirloom sewing, smocking and embroidery, and precious moments with her family.

STENCILLED CUSHION

Designed and made by Stephanie Simes

Sunshine bright, this painted and embroidered cushion will light up the dullest corner.

MATERIALS

24 cm (9½ in) square of prewashed calico

5 cm (2 in) wide fabric for the first border

17 cm (6¾ in) wide fabric for the second border

45 cm (18 in) of fabric for the backing

Three large buttons

FolkArt Acrylic Colors: Calico Red 932, Harvest Gold 917, Bluegrass 916

Small stanley knife

Small stencil brush

Three Manila folders

DMC Stranded Cotton: Red 321, Yellow 725, Green 502

Crewel needle, size 7

Two medium-sized red buttons

Egg carton

40 cm (16 in) cushion insert

Pencil

PREPARATION

See the design on the Pull Out Pattern Sheet.

STEP ONE

Photocopy three copies of the design. Place the first copy on the open Manila folder. Trace over the stems only, using the pencil and pressing firmly. The outline will be visible on the Manila folder. Using the stanley knife, cut out the stems from the Manila folder.

STEP TWO

Repeat the same process, using the second copy and another Manila folder, tracing and cutting out the shape of the yellow flowers and the yellow buds in the centre flower.

STEP THREE

Repeat the process, using the third copy and the last Manila folder, for the red flowers you now have three stencils.

STENCILLING

STEP ONE

Centre the stem stencil on the fabric. Load the brush with the Bluegrass, then dab most of the paint off onto the egg carton. This will help prevent the paint bleeding under the stencil and, at the same time, will give that slightly faded look. To stencil, use a stabbing movement up and down inside the cut-out, until you are satisfied that it is all painted. Allow the paint to dry before the next step.

STEP TWO

Using the Calico Red and the appropriate stencil, stencil the red flowers, then using Harvest Gold and the appropriate stencil, stencil the yellow flowers. Make sure your brush is thoroughly washed and dried between colours and that each colour is dry before proceeding to the next one. When changing colours, carefully line up the stencil, so there is no overlap.

STEP THREE

Set the paint by pressing with a hot iron, using a pressing cloth.

EMBROIDERY

Using one strand of Green cotton, outline the stems in herringbone stitch. Using one strand of Yellow cotton, outline the yellow flowers in blanket stitch. Using one strand of Red cotton, outline the red flowers in blanket stitch.

MAKING UP

STEP ONE

Wash and iron all the fabrics before you begin sewing. Cut the fabric for the first border into 4.5 cm (1¾ in) wide strips. Sew the first border around the calico square, measuring against the square and ironing and cutting each side before commencing the next.

STEP TWO

Cut the fabric for the second border into 8.5 cm (3¼ in) wide strips. Sew the second border around the calico square in the same way as for the first border. Sew on the red buttons.

STEP THREE

Cut the backing fabric the same size as the cushion front. Cut two strips, 9 cm (3½ in) wide, of the backing fabric for the facing. With the right sides together, stitch the facings to the top of the cushion front and the cushion back. Neaten the other end of the facings with a small hem. Turn the facings toward the inside and press well.

STEP FOUR

Place the cushion front and the back together with the right sides facing. Sew around three sides, leaving the top unstitched.

STEP FIVE

Handstitch three buttonholes to match the size of the buttons you have chosen, then sew on the buttons to correspond. Slip the cover over the cushion insert.

SMOCKED DRESS

Designed and stitched by Stephanie Simes

Your little angel will look heavenly in this party-perfect dress.

To fit: 4-5 years

MATERIALS

2.2 m (2¹/₂ yd) of cream fabric
30 cm (12 in) of iron-on interfacing
DMC Perle 8 Cotton, Ecru
Crewel needle, size 7
1 m (1¹/₈ yd) of cream silk organza
Narrow elastic
Three small buttons
1 m (1¹/₈ yd) of cream satin mini piping
Cream bias binding
50 cm (20 in) of narrow cream ribbon
Ordinary sewing cotton, Cream

PREPARATION

See the smocking graph on page 12 and the pattern on the Pull Out Pattern Sheet.

STEP ONE

The front of the dress is stitched in one piece – there are no joins. To determine the length of fabric to be smocked, measure your child from the top of the neck to the desired length. This will allow for some shrinkage caused by the smocking. This will be the length of your front piece. Most fabrics are 115 cm (45 in) wide – this will be the width of your dress. Cut a piece of fabric to these measurements.

STEP TWO

Use a smocking machine or iron-on dots to gather up the fabric for smocking. For a size four, you will need to gather sixteen full rows; for size five, gather eighteen full rows.

SMOCKING

Note: On the smocking graph, the dark horizontal lines are the gathering threads. The light horizontal lines are the space intervals between the gathering threads – the guides for spacing threads. Each vertical line represents a pleat. The slanted lines or slashes indicate where a pleat will be picked. All stitches are worked from left to right. Left-handers should turn the work upside down to work. Always leave the first and last row of gathering thread unsmocked.

STEP ONE

Stitch the smocking in DMC Perle 8 Cotton, following the graph.

STEP TWO

When the smocking is completed, pull out the gathering threads and block the garment to the size of your pattern.

MAKING UP

STEP ONE

Stay-stitch the neckline and sleeve lines, then cut out the neckline and armholes. Cut the rest of the dress from the fabric, except for the sleeves. Cut the sleeves from the silk organza.

STEP TWO

Cut two back yokes on the fold. Press the centre fold. Open out the left back yoke and, using the cream ribbon working from the inside to the outside, stitch three loops to accommodate the buttons you have selected. Cut two back yokes from the iron-on interfacing. Fuse the interfacing to the wrong side of the yokes.

STEP THREE

Finish the centre back of the two back skirt pieces with overlocking or zigzag stitching. Sew the centre back seam, leaving it open 8 cm (3¹/₈ in) from the top edge. Press the seam open.

STEP FOUR

Stitch two rows of gathering thread along the top of the back skirts (making sure you do not include the underarm edges in the gathering). Gather the back skirts to fit the back yokes. With the right sides together, sandwich the back skirts between the back yoke sections. Pin and stitch. Trim the seams, then turn the yoke/skirt right side out. Sew on the buttons to correspond with the loops.

STEP FIVE

Stitch the front to the back at the shoulder seams.

STEP SIX

Turn up and press a 5 cm (2 in) hem at the bottom of the sleeves. Measure around the child's arm and take 2.5 cm (1 in) from this measurement. Cut two pieces of elastic to that size. Stretching the elastic as you sew, stitch the elastic to the sleeve, using a wide zigzag stitch and fixing the hem in place as you go.

STEP SEVEN

Sew two rows of gathering stitches between the dots marked on the pattern. With right sides facing, stitch the underarm seam of the dress and the sleeves with a French seam. With the right sides of the sleeves and dress facing, gather the sleeves to fit the armholes. Pin, then stitch the sleeves into place. Press the seam toward the dress and topstitch the armholes, so the seam is caught in and is not visible.

STEP EIGHT

Cut the satin mini piping to fit the neckline. Sew the piping along the right side of the neckline, using the zipper foot on your sewing machine, 1.5 cm ($^5/_8$ in) from the edge. Cut the bias binding to fit the neckline, then sew it over the piping, following the same stitching line. Trim the edges, then turn the bias binding to the inside. Slipstitch the bias binding to the inside of the dress. Hem the dress to the desired length. Sew on the three small buttons to correspond with the loops.

Smocking is a charming feature on a dress for a little girl

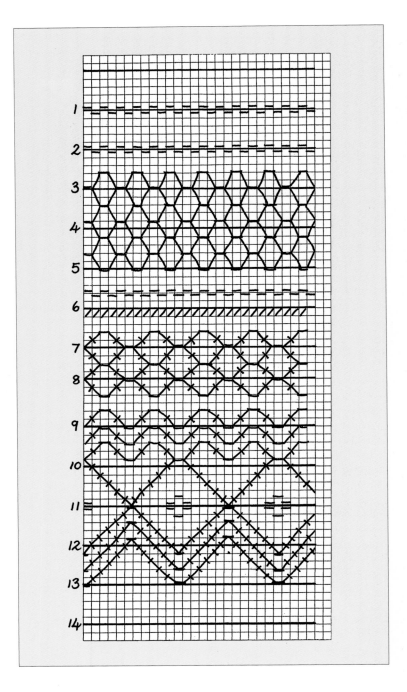

12

WEEKEND LOG CABIN

Designed by Carol Kinross and stitched by Stephanie Simes

Make this fabulous queen-size quilt in a weekend and transform your bedroom.

Finished size: approximately 250 cm (98 in) square

MATERIALS

Note: All fabric requirements are based on 115 cm (45 in) wide fabric.

30 cm (12 in) of fabric for the centre
50 cm (20 in) of fabric for Rows 2 and 3
65 cm (26 in) of fabric for Rows 4 and 5
95 cm (38 in) of fabric for Rows 6 and 7
120 cm (47 in) of fabric for Rows 8 and 9
120 cm (47 in) of fabric for Rows 10 and 11

120 cm (47 in) of fabric for Rows 12 and 13
110 cm (44 in) of fabric for the first border (optional)
120 cm (47 in) of fabric for the second border (optional)
7.8 m (8½ yd) of backing fabric (or the appropriate amount of sheeting to suit the finished size)
Wadding to suit the finished size
85 cm (33½ in) of fabric for the binding
Sewing thread
Quilting thread
Olfa cutter
Self-healing cutting mat and ruler

Note: Read all the instructions carefully, before you begin.

CUTTING

STEP ONE

Cut off all selvages. Cut 140 mm (5½ in) wide strips across the width of the fabrics for Rows 2 to 13, then cut the desired length.

STEP TWO

For the centres, cut four 266 mm (10½ in) squares. You should be able to cut four squares across the width of the fabric. If your fabric is not 115 cm (45 in) wide or your selvage is very wide, divide

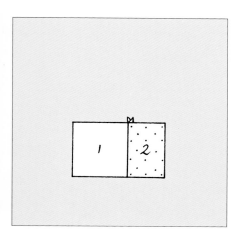

Fig. 1

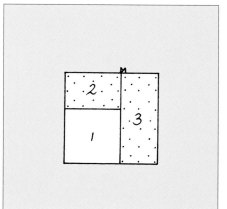

Fig. 2

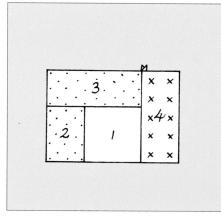

Fig. 3

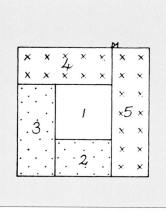

Fig. 4

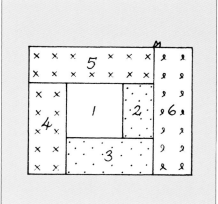

Fig. 5

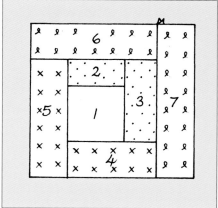

Fig. 6

the usable width of fabric by four and make this the size of the centre square. If you make adjustments here, you will need to make the appropriate adjustments to all the other measurements.

STEP THREE

Cut the following lengths from the strips: For Row 2, cut four 266 mm (10$^1\!/\!_2$ in); for Row 3, cut four 394 mm (15$^1\!/\!_2$ in); for Row 4, cut four 394 mm (15$^1\!/\!_2$ in); for Row 5, cut four 520 mm (20$^1\!/\!_2$ in); for Row 6, cut four 520 mm (20$^1\!/\!_2$ in); for Row 7, cut four 648 mm (25$^1\!/\!_2$ in); for Row 8, cut four 648 mm (25$^1\!/\!_2$ in); for Row 9, cut four 775 mm (30$^1\!/\!_2$ in); for Row 10, cut four 775 mm (30$^1\!/\!_2$ in); for Row 11, cut four 900 mm (35$^1\!/\!_2$ in); for Row 12, cut four 900 mm (35$^1\!/\!_2$ in); for Row 13, cut four 1028 mm (40$^1\!/\!_2$ in).

STEP FOUR

For the first border, cut seven 140 mm (5$^1\!/\!_2$ in) wide strips across the width of

the fabric. For the second border, cut eight 140 mm (5$^1\!/\!_2$ in) wide strips across the width of the fabric.

STEP FIVE

For the binding, cut ten 76 mm (3 in) wide strips across the width of the fabric. Cut off the selvages.

MAKING UP

STEP ONE

Piece the four Log Cabin blocks, following figures 1 to 12. Join the blocks together, matching the centre seams.

STEP TWO

For the first border, join the strips. Attach the top and bottom borders, then the sides. Press. Attach the second border in the same way. Press.

STEP THREE

Cut off the selvages, then cut the backing into three sections. Rejoin them on the long sides to make one large piece 260 cm (102 in) long. Lay the prepared backing wrong side up with the wadding on top, making sure there are no creases or pleats in the backing. Place the quilt top, right side up, on top of the wadding. Carefully pin or baste the layers together. Quilt as desired.

STEP FOUR

Join the binding strips three at a time – any more makes a very long strip which is very difficult to handle. With the wrong sides facing, fold the strips over double. Pin the binding to the right side of the top and bottom of the quilt with the raw edges matching. Turn the binding to the back of the quilt and slipstitch it in place. Bind the sides in the same way.

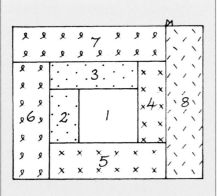
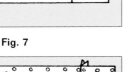

Fig. 7

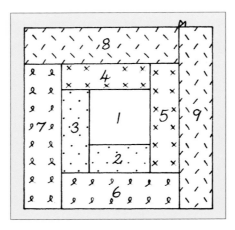

Fig. 8

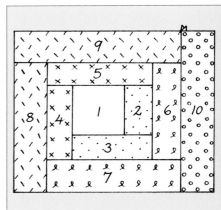

Fig. 9

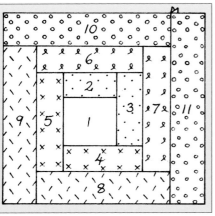

Fig. 10

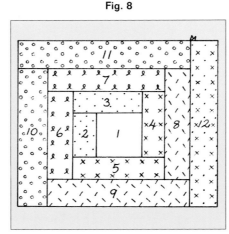

Fig. 11

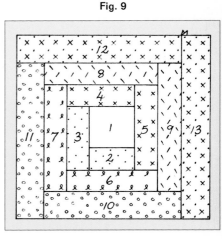

Fig. 12

14

SCARECROW HEDGE

Designed and made by Annette Phelps

**A cheeky scarecrow guards this arrangement of dried
cottage flowers from marauding birds.**

MATERIALS

Fence post container approximately
   12 cm x 35 cm (5 in x 14 in)
One bunch each of larkspur, lavender,
   pink daisies (dried)
Four hydrangea stems
Ten to twelve dried roses
Gum twigs with leaves
20 cm (8 in) scarecrow
Dry foam to fit the container
40 cm (16 in) piece of rope or twine
Glue gun
Fine wire

MAKING UP

STEP ONE

Cut the foam to suit the box, then glue
the foam into the box.

STEP TWO

Starting at the back of the foam, layer
30-35 cm (12-14 in) pieces of larkspur
and lavender together. Start in the
middle, working out to the sides,
stopping approximately 5 cm (2 in)
from the outer edge.

STEP THREE

Cut the roses approximately 5-7 cm
(2-2³/₄ in) shorter than the lavender.
Place the roses in front of the previous
row, taking the roses around the sides
to the back of the box.

STEP FOUR

Place the daisies in the same way as
the roses, leaving space on one side to
glue in the scarecrow.

STEP FIVE

Cut the hydrangeas into flowerettes
and place them around the top of the
box, taking them around the sides.
Fill in the spaces at the back with the
leftover hydrangeas and gum twigs.
Twist the rope into a bow and attach
with the fine wire.

PATCHWORK AND CROSS STITCH QUILT

Designed by Stephanie Simes, stitched by Stephanie Simes and Jenny Taylor

Combining two old favourites in patchwork and cross stitch, this country-style quilt is sure to please.

Finished size: 164 cm (65 in) square

MATERIALS

1 m (1¹⁄₈ yd) of camel-coloured Klostern
Chenille needle, size 20
DMC Stranded Cotton, Green 935
80 cm (32 in) of camel-coloured fabric
Embroidery hoop
30 cm (12 in) of fabrics 1, 2, 7 and 9
40 cm (16 in) of fabrics 3, 6, 8 and 10
50 cm (20 in) of fabric 4
4.3 m (4²⁄₃ yd) of fabric 5 (includes binding and backing fabric)
80 cm (32 in) of fabric 11 (main fabric)
165 cm (65 in) of wadding
Ordinary sewing cotton

PREPARATION

See the embroidery designs on page 18 and the placement diagram on page 21.

STEP ONE

Wash all the fabrics except the Klostern. Allow them to dry, then press.

STEP TWO

Cut nine squares of the Klostern, 46 squares x 46 squares. Cut nine same-sized squares of the camel-coloured fabric. Sew the camel fabric squares to the back of the Klostern, using a zigzag stitch around the edges.

EMBROIDERY

Find the centre of each Klostern square and mark it with a horizontal and vertical row of basting. Place a square in the hoop. Using six strands of the DMC 935 and the chenille needle, stitch the design, working one cross per square block marked on the Klostern. Stitch all nine squares.

MAKING UP

STEP ONE

For easier piecing, cut all the fabric (except the backing fabric) into 7.5 cm (3 in) wide strips along the length of the fabric.

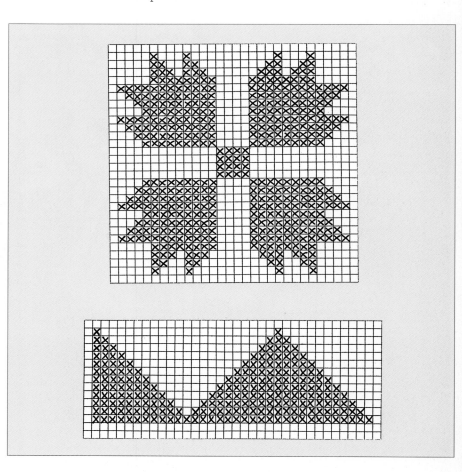

STEP TWO

Following the placement diagram on page 21, piece the blocks using a 6 mm ($^1/_4$ in) seam allowance throughout. Note that the order of piecing is indicated by the letters A to L and the fabric used is identified by numbers, 1 to 11.

STEP THREE

When the blocks are all pieced, assemble them in the arrangement shown in the placement diagram and join them together.

STEP FOUR

From the remaining Klostern cut five 7.5 cm (3 in) wide strips. You will have to join the strips together to achieve the desired size. Carefully join the strips, matching the squares of the fabric. Cut and attach the camel-coloured fabric to the back of the Klostern as before.

STEP FIVE

Stitch the Klostern borders to the quilt, making sure the edges are straight. Stitch the cross stitch design in the borders, using the same DMC thread as before, following the design graph.

STEP SIX

Cut the backing fabric to the size of the quilt top. Place the backing face down with the wadding on top, then the quilt top, face upwards. Baste the quilt with long stitches to hold the layers secure, then tie the quilt using six strands of DMC 935.

STEP SEVEN

Cut 7.5 cm (3 in) strips of binding fabric. Join strips to achieve the desired length. Fold the binding over double with the wrong sides together. Pin the binding to the right side of the quilt with the raw edges matching. Stitch the binding in place. Turn the folded edges to the back of the quilt and slipstitch them in place.

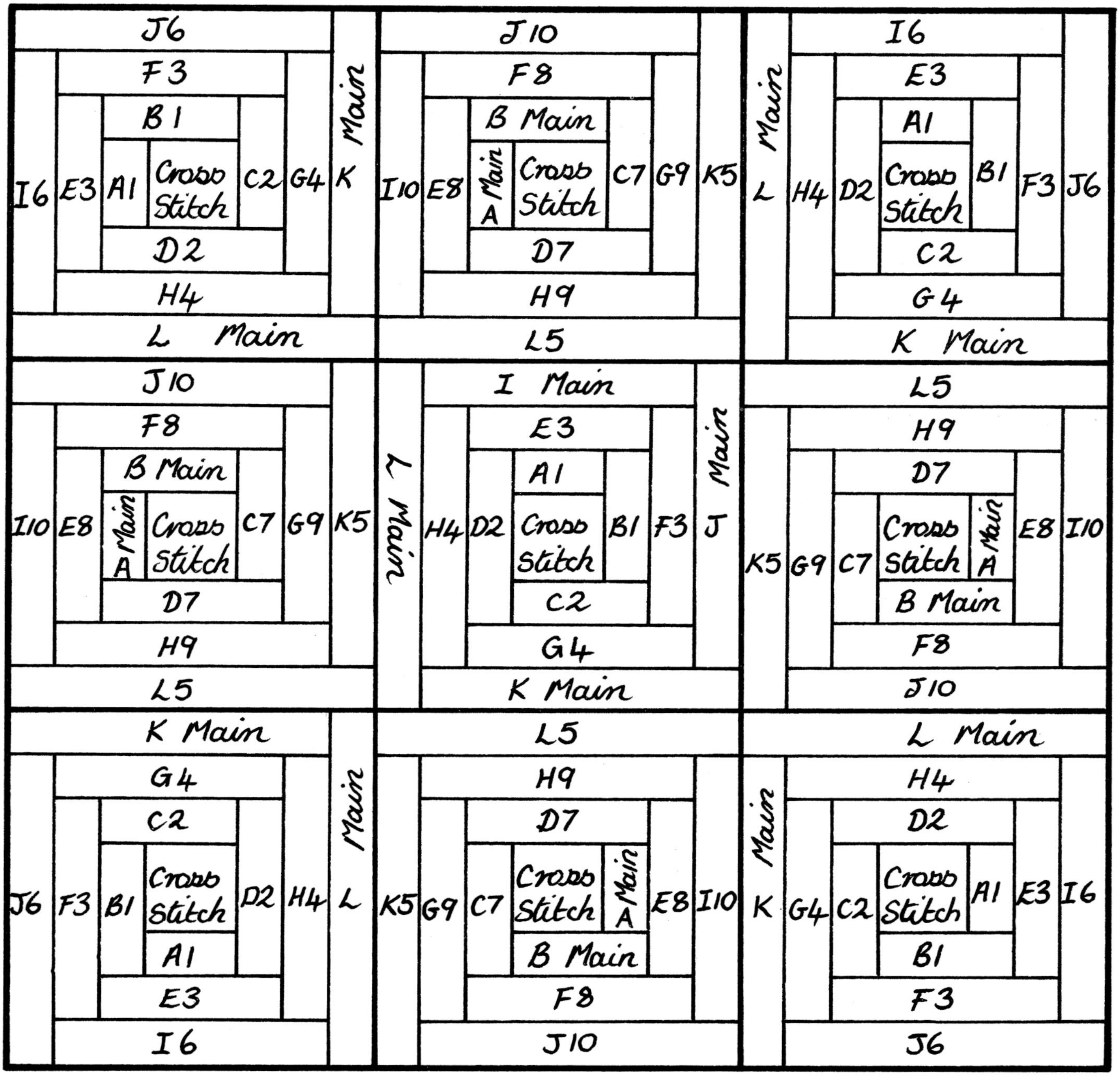

Block 1 (top-left):
J6 / F3 / B1 / I6 E3 A1 Cross Stitch C2 G4 K / D2 / H4 / L Main

Block 2 (top-center):
J10 / F8 / B Main / I10 E8 A Main Cross Stitch C7 G9 K5 / D7 / H9 / L5

Block 3 (top-right):
I6 / E3 / A1 / Main L H4 D2 Cross Stitch B1 F3 J6 / C2 / G4 / K Main

Block 4 (middle-left):
J10 / F8 / B Main / I10 E8 A Main Cross Stitch C7 G9 K5 / D7 / H9 / L5

Block 5 (middle-center):
I Main / E3 / A1 / L Main H4 D2 Cross Stitch B1 F3 J / C2 / G4 / K Main

Block 6 (middle-right):
L5 / H9 / D7 / K5 G9 C7 Cross Stitch A Main E8 I10 / B Main / F8 / J10

Block 7 (bottom-left):
K Main / G4 / C2 / J6 F3 B1 Cross Stitch D2 H4 L Main / A1 / E3 / I6

Block 8 (bottom-center):
L5 / H9 / D7 / K5 G9 C7 Cross Stitch A Main E8 I10 / B Main / F8 / J10

Block 9 (bottom-right):
L Main / H4 / D2 / Main K G4 C2 Cross Stitch A1 E3 I6 / B1 / F3 / J6

Placement Diagram

21

TEXTURED BLANKET

Designed and stitched by Stephanie Simes

A garland of wool-embroidered flowers adorns the front of this blanket,
providing a surprising contrast with the patchwork backing.

Finished size: 122 cm x 156 cm
(48 in x 61¾ in)

MATERIALS

110 cm x 160 cm (44 in x 63 in) of
Onkaparinga wool blanketing
122 cm x 156 cm (48 in x 61¾ in) of
thin wadding
160 cm (63 in) of fabric for the
borders
Fabric for the binding
Scraps of fabric for making the
pieced backing
Tapestry needles, assorted sizes
18-24
Little Wood Variegated Fleece Yarns:
Claret 17, Green/Brown 6
Little Wood Variegated Fleece Yarns
Gossamer/Mohair, Dark Green 4
Little Wood Fleece Yarns 2/22's:
Burgundy 6138, Yellow 255
Au Ver à Soie Antique Silk Thread,
Gold 222
Au Ver à Soie: Soie Perlee, Black
Mill Hill Petite Beads: Gold 40557,
Purple 02025
Kirra Yarns 4-ply: Purples 406, 407,
423; Yellow 111
4 m (4½ yd) of 3 mm (³⁄₁₆ in) wide
silk ribbon, Cream
2 m (2¼ yd) of 3 mm (³⁄₁₆ in) wide
silk ribbon, Olive Green
3 m (3³⁄₈ yd) of 3 mm (³⁄₁₆ in) wide
silk ribbon, Lavender
2 m (2¼ yd) of 7 mm (⁵⁄₁₆ in) wide
silk ribbon, Olive Green
2 m (2¼ yd) of 12 mm (½ in) wide
sparkling organza ribbon, 32
Torokina Yarn: Purples 225, 232

DMC Medici Wool: Greens 8406, 8411
DMC Stranded Cotton: Greens 501,
3012; Yellow Gold 834
Dark sewing thread for basting
Down Under Overdyed Wool, Blue/
Green 14
Blue water-soluble marker pen
(optional)
Variety of old buttons
Invisible thread

PREPARATION

See the embroidery design on the Pull
Out Pattern Sheet.

STEP ONE

Photocopy the design. You may have
to do this in sections, then join them
together. Cut away the paper on
the inside and outside of the wreath.
Centre the wreath shape on the wool
blanketing and pin it in place.

STEP TWO

Using a fine tapestry needle and dark
sewing thread, baste around the
wreath, inside and out, then remove
the paper.

STEP THREE

To transfer the design, cut out each
flower separately and carefully position and baste around it. Alternatively,
you could trace around the cut-out
pieces with the blue water-soluble
marker pen.

EMBROIDERY

STEP ONE

Cut and baste around the cosmos
(flower 1 on the pattern). There are
four of these – two large open blooms,
a bud and a half-open bloom at the top
right of the wreath. These are all
stitched in the same way. Using Little
Wood 17, satin stitch the petals, making
sure you follow the lines of the flower,
taking special care to change direction
in the bud. Stitch the centres in colonial
knots using Little Wood 6. Sew on
40557 beads randomly in the centres.
Using Little Wood 2/22-255, mixed
with one strand of Au Ver à Soie 222,
blanket stitch around the flowers with
approximately three stitches to every
petal. Stem stitch around the outside of
the flowers and the bud, using the Little
Wood 2/22-6138. With the Little Wood 6,
stitch the leaves in fishbone stitch.

STEP TWO

For flower 2, using the Down Under
Overdyed Wool and starting from the
centre, stitch a series of colonial knots
to form a circle, then stitch the overlapping petals in blanket stitch. To stitch
the stems, mix one strand of Au Ver à
Soie 222, one strand of DMC Medici
Wool 8411 and one strand of DMC
Stranded Cotton 3012. Stitch the bud in
blanket stitch, the stems in stem stitch
and the leaves in fishbone stitch.

23

STEP THREE

For flower 2b, stitch the same way as for flower 2, but stitch the leaves, stems and buds in two strands of DMC Medici Wool 8406.

STEP FOUR

For flower 3, stitch the centre in detached buttonhole stitch, using two strands of Torokina 232. This flower is stitched the same way you would stitch a bullion daisy. Start with three detached buttonholes stitches at the centre, then with each colour change, work a round of stitches until the circle is covered. The first round is stitched in one strand of Kirra 407, the second round is stitched in one strand of Kirra 406. For the stems, mix one strand of DMC Medici Wool 8411 and one strand of DMC Stranded Cotton 3012, using straight stitch for the bud and stem stitch for the stem.

STEP FIVE

For flower 4, stitch a series of colonial knots, using one strand of Kirra 111 to form the flower centres. Using the Cream silk ribbon, stitch the daisies in lazy daisy stitch. Stitch the leaves in blanket stitch, using one strand of Little Wood Gossamer/Mohair 4.

STEP SIX

For flower 5a (lavender), stitch in lazy daisy stitch in the lavender-coloured silk ribbon, commencing at the top of the bud and working to the bottom. Widen the bud slightly in the centre, then taper the bud towards the bottom. Using Torokina 225 and Black Au Ver à Soie, randomly stitch a series of fly stitches, following the lines of the lavender. To complete the flower, sew on the Mill Hill Petite Beads 02025 throughout the flower. For the foliage, stitch the leaves in lazy daisy stitch using the sparkling organza ribbon. Randomly stitch in fly stitch between the leaves, using one strand of DMC 501.

STEP SEVEN

For flower 5b, work the same as for 5a except for the foliage which is stitched in a series of lazy daisy stitches, using the Olive Green silk ribbon.

STEP EIGHT

For flower 6, stitch a series of colonial knots using six strands of DMC Stranded Cotton 834, to form the centre of the flower. Using detached buttonhole stitch and one strand of Kirra 111, stitch the flower petals. For the foliage, couch the stems behind the flowers, using one strand of Little Wood Gossamer/Mohair 4.

STEP NINE

For flower 7a, stitch the flower centres in straight stitches, using one strand of Torokina 232. For the next round, work a lazy daisy stitch around the previous stitch, using one strand of Kirra 423.

Repeat this step for the final round, using Kirra 406. Stitch the leaves and stems in blanket stitch, using six strands of DMC 501.

STEP TEN

For flower 7b, stitch the same as for flower 7a, except when stitching the foliage, stitch the stem in blanket stitch, using six strands of DMC 3012. Using the 7 mm ($^5/_{16}$ in) wide Olive Green silk ribbon, stitch three stitches close together, all coming from the same hole at the bottom and radiating out-

The patchwork back

wards at the top. Using one strand of the DMC 3012, catch the ribbon in with a small running stitch around the outside of the leaf, forming a leaf shape. With the same thread, stitch the veins of the leaf using fly stitch.

MAKING UP

STEP ONE

Remove all the basting threads. To make a scrap quilt for the back, wash all your selected fabrics, sew the scraps together in rows, then trim them to the same width. Join the rows to form a large rectangle. Using a rotary cutter or scissors, cut the rectangle into strips again, then rejoin them. You can repeat this as many times as you wish, until you are pleased with the effect.

STEP TWO

Cut the border fabric into 24 cm (9$^1/_2$ in) wide strips. Attach the side borders, then attach the top and bottom borders.

STEP THREE

Baste the pieced backing fabric to the back of the embroidered piece with the wadding in between. Cut 6 cm (2$^1/_2$ in) wide strips of the binding fabric. Join them, if necessary. Fold the binding over double with the wrong sides together, then stitch the binding to the sides of the blanket with the right sides facing and the raw edges even. Turn the binding to the back of the blanket and slipstitch it into place. Repeat for the top and bottom binding.

STEP FOUR

Every now and then, catch the three layers of the quilt together by stitching with invisible thread around the wreath area. Sew buttons on the back, but take care not to let the stitching show on the front.

HINTS

There is much controversy regarding the use of blue water-soluble marker pens. I am happy to use them, but I always follow these rules:

• Always pretest them on a piece of scrap fabric first.

• Never iron your project until it has been washed, as ironing will heat-set the marker.

• Remember that washing only with water removes the blue mark, but does not remove the chemical from the fabric. To do this, you must soak your project in cold water for five minutes, then wash it by hand, using lukewarm water and a mild soap, then rinse. While the piece is still damp, iron it dry on the wrong side of the work on top of a fluffy white towel. This will make the embroidery stand up.

• If you are using the marker pen on wool, try and draw your pattern slightly smaller than you will stitch it. This way, when you come to stitching, the wool will cover most of the blue marks.

• When washing wool, soak a white face washer in cold water with a wool wash dissolved in it. Dab the marks until they disappear. Wool wash does not need to be rinsed out, so this saves wear and tear on your blanketing.

If you are concerned about using these marker pens, the alternative is a 2B lead pencil. To remove pencil marks, wash the piece in lukewarm water with a mild soap. If the marks are still visible, use a fabric eraser or stale breadcrumbs (this may rub the fabric, so beware).

• When determining the correct size needle for a particular purpose, make sure the thread fits smoothly through the needle, sliding with ease.

Every now and again, move the position of the thread on the needle so it doesn't wear away the same spot on the thread.

• Measure the length of your third finger until slightly under your arm, then cut the thread to this length. Any longer and the thread will begin to knot and become unmanageable.

• Use beeswax if you are using two or more threads as it helps to keep them together and prevents tangles. The beeswax wears off while it is being worked through the fabric, and the residue can be washed out.

• Do not fold finished designs awaiting assembly, but instead, roll them on a cardboard cylinder.

25

CHRISTENING GOWN

Designed and stitched by Helen Redenbach

Generations to come will treasure this lovely gown with its matching petticoat.

MATERIALS

2.3 m (2¹/₂ yd) of Swiss voile
10.3 m (11¹/₄ yd) of insertion lace
1.8 m (2 yd) of entredeux
25 cm (10 in) of mini piping
5 m (5¹/₂ yd) of edging lace
Three tiny buttons
1.2 m (1¹/₃ yd) of fine satin ribbon
Two reels of heirloom thread
Madeira Silk Thread, White
Crewel embroidery needle, size 8
Straw needle, size 8

PREPARATION

See the pattern and the embroidery designs on the Pull Out Pattern Sheet.

STEP ONE

For the front skirt, cut the following pieces: one width of fabric 41 cm (16¹/₈ in) long, one width of fabric 12 cm (4³/₄ in) long, one width of fabric 14 cm (5¹/₂ in) long and one width of fabric 16 cm (6¹/₄ in) long.

STEP TWO

For the back skirt, cut the following pieces: one piece 41 cm x 90 cm (16¹/₈ in x 35¹/₂ in), one piece 12 cm x 90 cm (4³/₄ in x 35¹/₂ in), one piece 14 cm x 90 cm (5¹/₂ in x 35¹/₂ in), and one piece 16 cm x 90 cm (6¹/₄ in x 35¹/₂).

STEP THREE

Cut a piece of fabric 40 cm wide x 52 cm long (15³/₄ in wide x 20³/₈ in long). This will be used for the front and sleeves, after insertions are completed. Do not cut the front and sleeves at this point.

STEP FOUR

Cut the back yoke, following the pattern. Cut the back placket 4 cm x 17 cm (1¹/₄ in x 6³/₄ in). Cut a piece of bias fabric for the neck binding 2 cm x 30 cm (³/₄ in x 12 in).

SMOCKING

On the 41 cm (16¹/₈ in) long front skirt piece, pleat ten full rows, including two holding rows. Take out 5 cm (2 in) of pleats at each side to allow for the armhole shaping (Fig. 1). Smock, following the smocking pattern, using two strands of Madeira Silk Thread.

LACE INSERTION

Note: All the lace is inserted using the 'roll and whip' method.

Using the buttonhole foot, set the sewing machine to zigzag (width 3, length ³/₄-1, needle position left). Place the fabric right side down and stitch so the needle catches the fabric and clears the raw edge. Using the buttonhole foot and zigzag stitch, butt the rolled and whipped edge of the fabric to the lace (both right sides up). Adjust the width of the zigzag so the needle will catch the edge of fabric on one side and the lace heading on the other side. The length of the stitch should be fairly short.

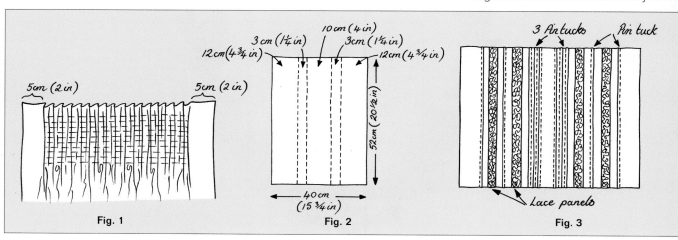

Fig. 1   Fig. 2   Fig. 3

FRONT BODICE

STEP ONE

Make the lace insertion panel for the front bodice in the following way. Using the 40 cm wide x 52 cm long (15³/₄ in wide x 20³/₈ in long) fabric, pull a thread at 12 cm (4³/₄ in) across, then 3 cm (1¹/₄ in) away, then 10 cm (4 in) away, then 3 cm (1¹/₄ in) away, leaving another 12 cm (4³/₄ in) space at the other end (Fig. 2). Carefully cut the fabric along the pulled threads and insert four panels of lace using the described method.

STEP TWO

On the same piece, work pintucks approximately 1 cm (³/₈ in) from each lace panel plus an extra two rows 5 mm (¹/₄ in) from the two centre pin tucks (Fig. 3).

STEP THREE

For the front bodice, measure 15 cm (5⁷/₈ in) down the length of the panel with the lace and pintucks and cut across at this point. Find the centre of the piece, pull a thread then slit the piece in half. Roll and whip both centre edges. From the leftover voile, cut a triangle with a base of 9 cm (3¹/₄ in) and 12 cm (4³/₄ in) high. Roll and whip the two 12 cm (4³/₄ in) sides (Fig. 4).

STEP FOUR

Trim the fabric edge from the side of the entredeux. Butt the entredeux to the rolled and whipped edges of the front bodice, then zigzag them together as for the lace. Make sure you adjust the length of the zigzag so the 'zig' catches the rolled hem and the 'zag' goes into each hole of the entredeux. Remove the other fabric edge from the entredeux, then join it to one side of the triangle in the same way. Repeat for the other side of the triangle (Fig. 5). Using the pattern provided, cut out the front bodice.

SLEEVES

Cut the remaining lace panel in half lengthwise. Find the centre, pull a thread and slit down the centre, as before. Roll and whip the centre edges. Insert the entredeux as for the bodice using triangles with a 9 cm (3¹/₂ in) base and a height of 16 cm (6¹/₄ in). Cut out the sleeves using the pattern provided.

MAKING UP

STEP ONE

Block the smocking, then using the pattern provided, cut an armhole from each side of the smocking. Stitch a length of the mini piping to the right side of the lower edge of the front bodice with the raw edges matching. You may find this easier if you use the zipper foot on your sewing machine. With the right sides facing, baste the front bodice to the smocked skirt panel, ensuring the mini piping lies just above the first row of smocking. Stitch. Trim the seam and zigzag the raw edges.

Find the centre back at the top edge of the 41 cm x 90 cm (16¹/₈ in x 35¹/₂ in) back skirt piece and cut down 8 cm (3¹/₈ in) for the back placket. Staystitch close to the slit, pivoting at the lowest point. With the right sides facing, stitch the placket to the opening.

Press the seam allowance away from the seam. Press under the seam allowance on the other side of the placket. Fold the placket over to the wrong side and slipstitch the folded edge in place.

STEP THREE

Using the pattern provided, cut out the armhole shaping at both sides.

STEP FOUR

Stitch two rows of gathering thread across the top edge, breaking the stitching at the placket. Pull up the gathering to fit the back yokes. Leaving the left placket out and folding the right placket to the inside, join the back bodices to the back skirt, with the right sides facing and with the fold lines of the bodices aligned with the edges of the placket (Fig. 6).

Pintucks and insertion lace complete the bodice

STEP FIVE

Finish the edge of the bodice facings. Fold the facings around the skirt. Stitch, trim the seam and zigzag the edges. Press the facings to the inside.

STEP SIX

Join the shoulder seams, using fine French seams. Sew two rows of gathering across the heads of the sleeves. Sew the sleeves to the garment, using fine French seams. Roll and whip the bottom edges of the sleeves. Attach a length of entredeux to the bottom of the sleeves, then attach the lace edging.

STEP SEVEN

With the right sides facing, stitch the bias strip to the neck. Press the strip towards the neck opening. Press under the seam allowance on the other raw edge. The finished bias should be about 5 mm (^{1}/$_4$ in) wide. Turn the bias in at the centre backs and around the neck and slipstitch it in place.

STEP EIGHT

Join the side seams of the top skirt, bodice and sleeves, using fine French seams. Join the side seams of the other three skirt panels, using fine French seams. Roll and whip the raw edge at the bottom of the top skirt. Attach the insertion lace. Roll and whip the top

edge of the 12 cm (4^3/$_4$ in) skirt panel. Join it to the lace, making sure you align the side seams. Continue down the skirt, insert the lace, then add the 14 cm (5^1/$_2$ in) skirt panel, then insertion lace, then the 16 cm (6^1/$_4$ in) skirt panel, then insertion lace. Gather the lace edging and carefully zigzag it to the last row of insertion lace.

STEP NINE

Make three small buttonholes on the right back yoke. Attach the three buttons on the left back yoke to correspond with the buttonholes. Thread the fine satin ribbon through the entredeux in the sleeves and tie bows.

EMBROIDERY

Note: Use one strand of the Madeira Silk Thread for all the embroidery.

STEP ONE

Work a row of bullion roses in each diamond across the top of the smocking and in every fourth diamond on the second row from the bottom of the smocking.

STEP TWO

On the front bodice, work three bullion roses plus buds and leaves in the centre of the bodice. On the sleeves, work one bullion rose plus buds and leaves in the centre of each sleeve.

STEP THREE

In the centre of the second skirt panel, work five bullion roses plus leaves and buds in a curve. In the next panel, work five bullion roses plus leaves and buds in a row at an angle to the hem. Work a similar group on the bottom panel with seven bullion roses, maintaining the angle (Fig. 7).

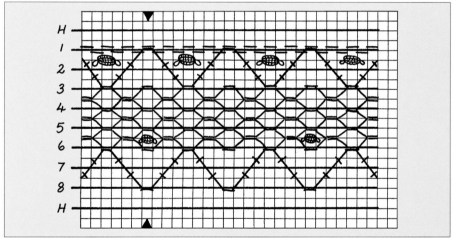

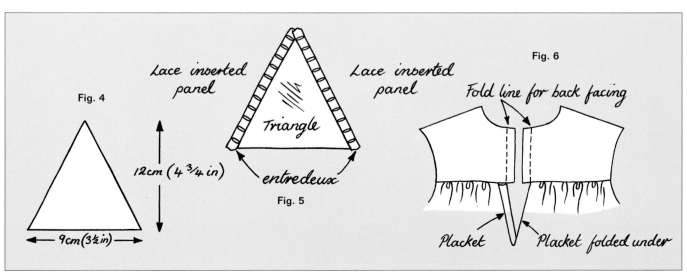

Fig. 4

12cm (4 3/4 in)

9cm (3½ in)

Lace inserted panel

Triangle

Lace inserted panel

entredeux

Fig. 5

Fig. 6

Fold line for back facing

Placket

Placket folded under

29

PETTICOAT

MATERIALS

1 m (1$\frac{1}{8}$ yd) of 150 cm (60 in) wide batiste
Two small buttons
One reel of heirloom thread
Twin needle

CUTTING

Cut one front skirt 82 cm wide x 85 cm long (32 in wide x 33$\frac{1}{2}$ in long) and one back skirt 60 cm wide x 85 cm long (24 in wide x 33$\frac{1}{2}$ in long). Using the same pattern pieces as for the christening gown, cut two front bodices and two back bodices on the fold as indicated. Cut one back placket piece 4 cm x 17 cm (1$\frac{1}{2}$ in x 6$\frac{3}{4}$ in) and a bias strip for binding the armholes 2 cm x 30 cm ($\frac{3}{4}$ in x 12 in).

MAKING UP

STEP ONE

Press in the fold line on each bodice back. With the right sides facing, join one front bodice to one left and right back bodice at the shoulders, taking care not to catch the facings (Fig. 8). Join the other front bodice to the back facings at the shoulders. Trim the seams and press flat.

STEP TWO

Slit up the seam allowance at the centre back folds. Press the seam allowance up on the front and both back bodice facings.

STEP THREE

With the right sides together, fold the back bodices at the fold line, matching the shoulder seams and the centre fronts. Stitch around the neck edge. Matching the shoulder seams, stitch around the armholes (Fig. 9). Trim the seams and clip the curves. Turn the bodice to the right side and press.

STEP FOUR

Using the armhole guide, cut out the shaping in the front and back skirts. At the centre back skirt, make a placket as for the christening gown.

STEP FIVE

Join the side seams using fine French seams.

STEP SIX

Stitch the bias strips to the armholes, with the right side of the bias strip to the wrong side of the armhole and using a 5 mm ($\frac{1}{4}$ in) seam allowance. Fold over the bias and stitch, forming a 5 mm ($\frac{1}{4}$ in) finished binding.

STEP SEVEN

Sew two rows of gathering across the tops of the skirts. Pull up the gathering to fit the bodice. With the right sides facing and keeping the bodice facing clear, join the bodice to the skirt. Trim the seams. Slipstitch the folded edge of the bodice facing over the seam.

STEP EIGHT

Work two small buttonholes on the right back bodice. Attach the two buttons on the left back to correspond.

STEP NINE

For the hem, press up and pin 1 cm ($\frac{3}{8}$ in), then 2 cm ($\frac{3}{4}$ in). Using the twin needle and working from the right side, sew around the hem, just below the top so the twin needles finish the hem. You will be able to see the turned up hem from the right side of the petticoat.

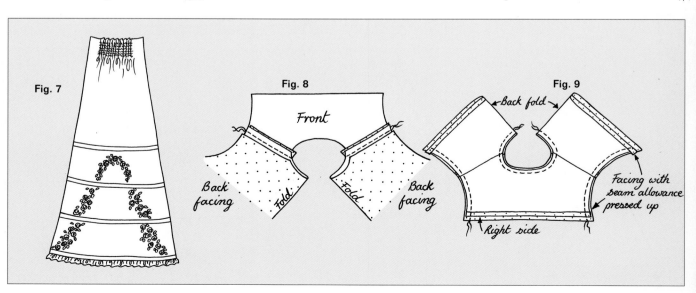

Fig. 7

Fig. 8 — Front — Back facing — Fold — Fold — Back facing

Fig. 9 — Back fold — Facing with seam allowance pressed up — Right side

TEDDY BEAR'S GARDEN

Designed and stitched by Jane Toohey

Teddy bears frolic in this embroidered garden which would make a delightful pillow, framed picture or little girl's pinafore.

MATERIALS

50 cm (20 in) square of striped cotton fabric

2B lead pencil

DMC Stranded Cotton: Greens 988, 3053, 3347, 3348, 3362, 3363, 3364; Pinks 778, 3688, 3726; Ecru; Beige 422; Blue 932; Lilac 3041; Yellow 744; Brown 642, 838, 839, 841, 938; Orange 352, 722; Grey 646; Blanc Neige

Crewel needles, assorted sizes

Straw needles, assorted sizes

Embroidery hoop (optional)

Masking tape

Note: For bullion stitch, use straw needles, but use crewel needles for all other stitching. As a general rule, use a size 8 for two strands of thread, a size 7 for three strands of thread, a size 6 for four and five strands of thread, and a size 5 for six strands of thread.

PREPARATION

See the embroidery design on the Pull Out Pattern Sheet.

Photocopy the embroidery design. Tape the photocopy to a window with the fabric on top. Using the pencil, lightly trace the design onto the fabric. Take care to centre the design, using the bottom of the heart shape on the gate as a guide.

EMBROIDERY

STEP ONE

For the gate, using three strands of 3041, stem stitch the gate outline. Stitch the two top circles in stem stitch in a circular pattern until the entire area has been filled in. Stitch the fence posts in eight rows of stem stitch. Stitch the path in stem stitch, using three strands of 646, mixed with one strand of 642.

STEP TWO

Stitch the hollyhocks in buttonhole stitch, using three strands of thread. Three shades of pink are used – a light pink 778 (marked with crosses), a medium pink 3688 and a dark pink 3726 (marked with circles). Stitch the bottom area of the flower in buttonhole stitch, using three strands of Blanc Neige. Stitch the leaves in buttonhole stitch, using four strands of 3362. Work stem stitch for the vein. Stitch the stems in four strands of 3363. Use this colour for the colonial knots at the top of the flowers.

STEP THREE

To stitch the fruit on the tree, use straight stitch in three strands of 722. Stitch the leaves in lazy daisy stitch, using one strand of 3364 with three strands of 3362. Fill in all the areas of foliage in lazy daisy stitch. Stitch the trunk in two rows of stem stitch in three strands of 839. Using six strands of 3041, stem stitch the fence beneath the tree.

STEP FOUR

Stitch the top of the pot in three rows of stem stitch, side by side, using six strands of 642. For the body of the pot, stem stitch two rows, side by side, beginning with 841, then sew two rows in the other direction in 642.

STEP FIVE

Stitch the cauliflower centres in approximately eleven colonial knots, using six strands of Ecru. Stitch a series of lazy daisy leaves, using six strands of 3348. Around these, stitch another lazy daisy stitch (directly over the previous one) using six strands of 988.

STEP SIX

Using two strands of Ecru, stem stitch the chook until the entire area has been filled in. Stitch the feet in stem stitch, using one strand of 744. Stitch the beak and the comb in straight stitch, using one strand of 352. Using two strands of 838, stitch a colonial knot for the eye.

STEP SEVEN

For the larger bear, use four strands of 422. The head, legs, body and arms are all stitched in separate sections. To stitch the head, start on the outside of the circle, chain stitching a complete circle, then commencing the next one inside the one just stitched. Work in this way until the face is filled. Stitch four small straight stitches in four strands of 838 for the nose. Stitch the eyes in colonial knots in four strands of 838. Stitch the feet in the same way as the head. Stitch the limbs, following the direction marked on the pattern. Stitch the shirt in chain stitch, using six strands of 3348, stitching in the direction of the lines.

STEP EIGHT

Stitch the smaller bear in the same way as the large bear. The shirt on the small bear is stitched in a stripe pattern, using six strands of 932 with six strands of Blanc Neige.

STEP NINE

Using four strands of 841 and beginning on the outside of the pram, work chain stitch in the direction of the lines marked on the pattern. Stitch the outline in Portuguese knot stitch (see Figs 1-5 below). Stitch the wheels in stem stitch, using three strands of 938. The wheels have two rows of stem stitch while the spokes have one row of stem stitch. Stitch a small circle stitched in stem stitch for the hubs. Stitch the handle of the pram in stem stitch in two rows of 938.

STEP TEN

Stitch the patchwork quilt in satin stitch in small blocks alternating six strands of the following colours: 3041, 3362, Blanc Neige, 932 and 3347.

STEP ELEVEN

Stitch the three bullion stitches in the centres of the cabbages, using four strands of 3348. Add bullion stitches on the sides and underneath the centre, using four strands of 3053.

STEP TWELVE

Wash out the pencil marks with mild soap and lukewarm water. Press the fabric while it is still damp, taking care not to flatten the embroidery.

STITCH GUIDE

STEM STITCH

Take a long stitch, bringing the needle out approximately half a stitch length back. Repeat this procedure along the required length, keeping the ribbon beneath the needle.

BUTTONHOLE STITCH

Working from left to right, pull the needle through the fabric over the top of the working thread. Stitches can be worked side by side or spaced.

CHAIN STITCH

Work chain stitch as shown in Fig. 1 and Fig. 2. When the row is complete take a small stitch over the last loop of the chain to secure it as shown in Fig. 3.

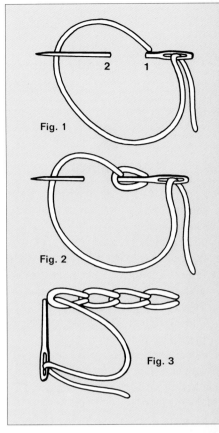

Chain stitch

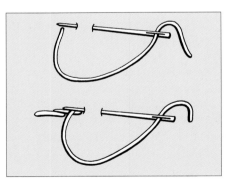

Stem stitch

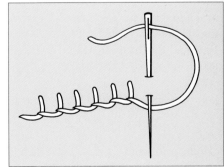

Buttonhole stitch

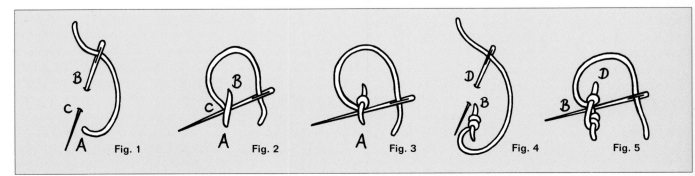

Portuguese knot stitch

COUNTRY WELCOME WALLHANGING

Designed and stitched by Carol Kinross

Welcome friends to your country cottage with this charming quilt.

Finished size: approximately 77 cm x 102 cm (30 in x 40 in)
Blocks: Twenty blocks 14 cm (5¹/₂ in) square

MATERIALS

Note: All fabric requirements are based on 115 cm (45 in) wide fabric.

60 cm (24 in) of fabric for the background
20 cm (8 in) of fabric for the main house (also used for the centre of the Log Cabin blocks)
35 cm (14 in) of fabric for the roof, chimneys, door and Rows 6 and 7 of the Log Cabin blocks
20 cm (8 in) of fabric for the windows and Rows 2 and 3 of the Log Cabin blocks
30 cm (12 in) of fabric for the grass and Rows 4 and 5 of the Log Cabin blocks
30 cm (12 in) of fabric for Rows 8 and 9 of the Log Cabin blocks
Scraps or 10 cm (4 in) of fabric for the blocks, trees and tree trunks

Scraps or 15 cm (6 in) of fabric for the hearts and 'Welcome'
Thin wadding or apparel wadding
85 cm (34 in) of fabric for the backing
35 cm (14 in) of fabric for the binding
Template plastic
Thread for piecing plus matching thread for appliqué and quilting thread (if required)
Blue water-soluble marker pen or pencil
Fray stopper (optional)

Note: Please read through the instructions carefully before you begin. Accurate cutting and sewing are essential for the pieces to fit together.

PREPARATION

See the templates on the Pull Out Pattern Sheet.

Trace the templates onto the template plastic and carefully cut them out. All seam allowances are 6 mm (¹/₄ in). Seam allowances are included on all templates and in all measurements, except the heart and letters templates. You must add your own seam allowances to hand-appliqué. Where possible, place the templates square on the fabric. Arrows indicate the fabric grain line.

LOG CABIN BLOCKS

STEP ONE

For Rows 1 and 2, cut twenty 38 mm (1¹/₂ in) squares of both colours. For Rows 3 and 4, cut twenty 38 mm x 65 mm (1¹/₂ in x 2¹/₂ in) rectangles from both colours. For Rows 5 and 6, cut twenty 38 mm x 90 mm (1¹/₂ in x 3¹/₂ in) rectangles from both colours. For Rows 7 and 8, cut twenty 38 mm x 115 mm (1¹/₂ in x 4¹/₂ in) rectangles of both colours. For Row 9, cut twenty 38 mm x 140 mm (1¹/₂ in x 5¹/₂ in) rectangles.

STEP TWO

Piece the Log Cabin blocks, following figures 1 to 8.

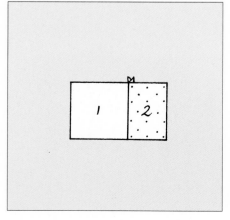

Fig. 1

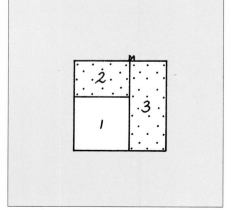

Fig. 2

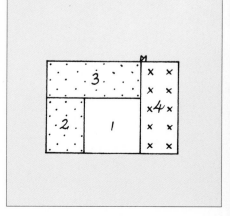

Fig. 3

HOUSE AND TREES

STEP ONE

Cut out the templates for the house and trees as indicated on the templates. Piece the house and the large tree, following figures 9 to 12.

STEP TWO

From the background fabric, cut two 38 mm x 90 mm (1$\frac{1}{2}$ in x 3$\frac{1}{2}$ in) rectangles for the base of the small tree. From the tree trunk fabric, cut two 32 mm x 38 mm (1$\frac{1}{4}$ in x 1$\frac{1}{2}$ in) rectangles for the small tree. Piece the small tree in the same sequence as the large tree, except that the trunk is appliquéd.

STEP THREE

From the background fabric, cut one 115 mm x 121 mm (4$\frac{1}{2}$ in x 4$\frac{3}{4}$ in) rectangle for above the large tree. Stitch it to the top of the pieced trees, then attach them to either side of the completed house section.

STEP FOUR

From the background fabric, cut a 90 mm x 235 mm (3$\frac{1}{2}$ in x 9$\frac{1}{4}$ in) rectangle for above the small tree. Stitch the rectangle to the top of the pieced small trees, then attach the trees to either side of the large tree/house section.

TO COMPLETE PIECING

STEP ONE

From the grass fabric, cut a 102 mm x 685 mm (4 in x 27 in) rectangle. Stitch it to the bottom of the pieced house and trees.

STEP TWO

From the background fabric, cut two 58 mm x 406 mm (2$\frac{1}{4}$ in x 16 in) rectangles. Stitch one to each side of the house/trees/grass section.

STEP THREE

From the background fabric, cut a 38 mm x 775 mm (1$\frac{1}{2}$ in x 30$\frac{1}{2}$ in) rectangle. Stitch it to the grass section.

STEP FOUR

From the background fabric, cut a 102 mm x 775 mm (4 in x 30$\frac{1}{2}$ in) rectangle. Stitch it to the top of the pieced section.

STEP FIVE

From the background fabric, cut four 140 mm (5$\frac{1}{2}$ in) squares for the corners of the quilt.

STEP SIX

Join six Log Cabin blocks (making sure they are all facing the right way). Make two sets of blocks. Attach them to the top and bottom of the quilt. Join four Log Cabin blocks with a corner square on both ends. Make two sets. Attach these to the sides of the quilt, matching corner seams.

APPLIQUE

STEP ONE

Cut out the hearts and 'Welcome' by tracing around the templates on the right side of the fabric. If you are hand-appliquéing, leave enough space for a seam allowance between the pieces. Turn under the fabric edge on the traced lines and baste, clipping into curves and corners where necessary.

STEP TWO

Centre the 'Welcome' by placing the 'c' in the centre of the quilt and spacing the rest of the letters from that point. Pin or baste the letters and hearts into place, then stitch them with small even slipstitches, overstitching on parts where fraying may occur (e.g. the centre of the hearts). Alternatively, use fray stopper on these points. When centring the hearts in the corners, don't forget to centre from the seam allowance, not from the edge.

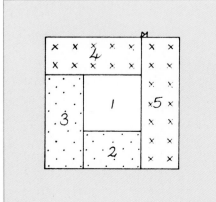

Fig. 4

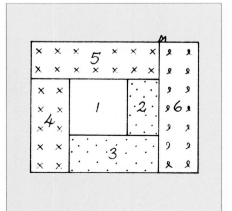

Fig. 5

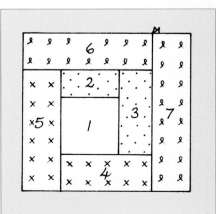

Fig. 6

MAKING UP

STEP ONE

Cut the backing fabric and wadding slightly bigger than the finished quilt top. Sandwich all three layers by carefully laying your backing fabric down, with the wrong side up; lay the wadding on top, taking care to keep backing smooth, then lay the quilt top (right side up) on the wadding.

STEP TWO

If you are machine-quilting, pin every 8-10 cm (3-4 in) using safety pins. If you are hand-quilting, hand-baste the layers together in a grid pattern with the rows 5-8 cm (2-3 in) apart. Quilt in your desired pattern.

BINDING

Cut four 75 mm (3 in) wide strips across the width of the fabric. Cut off the selvages. With the wrong sides facing, fold the strips over double. Pin the binding to the right side of the top and bottom of the quilt with the raw edges matching. Turn the binding to the back of the quilt and slipstitch it in place. Bind the sides in the same way.

HINTS

• You can use a rotary cutter for all of the cutting of the Log Cabin strips or they can be cut easily by hand.
• You can choose to wash your fabrics before you begin, if you are worried about colour fastness.

• Always test the water-soluble marker on your fabric to ensure that it does wash out. Do not press before you wash the marker out as this 'heat sets' the blue mark, making it permanent. It is very important that the marker be washed out properly when you have finished your project.
• You can appliqué by hand or by machine. Letters are not easy to appliqué. Be patient and careful. You can decide what method to use, depending on how much the fabric frays. If it frays a lot, machine-appliqué, if it doesn't, hand-appliqué.

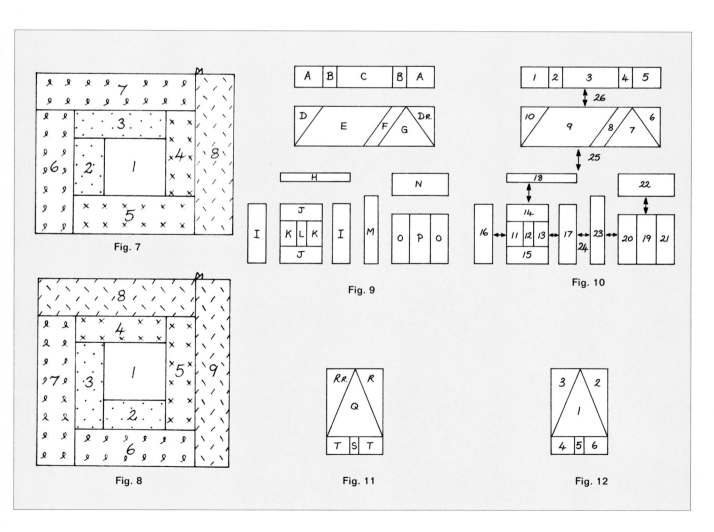

Fig. 7

Fig. 8

Fig. 9

Fig. 10

Fig. 11

Fig. 12

AFGHAN

Designed by Stephanie Simes, stitched by Jenny Taylor

Simplicity itself, this versatile afghan combines beauty and practicality. Throw it over the back of a chair for an instant decoration.

MATERIALS

125 cm (49 in) panel of Anne cloth (this will give you 6 squares x 9 squares)
Tapestry needle, size 24
DMC Stranded Cotton: Green 935, Dark Red 315

EMBROIDERY

See the embroidery graphs on page 38.

Note: There are six cross stitch designs in the afghan (Figs 1-6). Embroider them in the colour indicated in the position shown in the placement diagram. The designs are stitched over two threads of the Anne cloth, using three strands of the cotton. Because the work can be seen on the back, try to make all the stitches on the back horizontal and as neat as possible. Once the embroidery is completed, press the work on the wrong side.

STEP TWO

Trim the afghan to 5 cm (2 in) bigger than the six square by nine square finished size. Make the fringed border by drawing threads for a depth of 5 cm (2 in) on all sides. Tie each group of eight threads into a knot at the base.

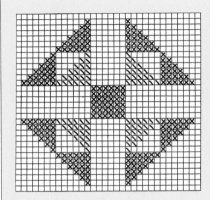
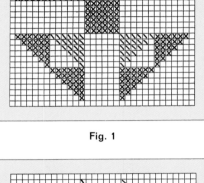

Fig. 1

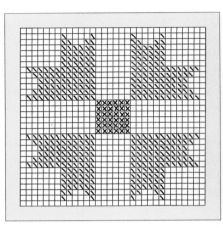

Fig. 2

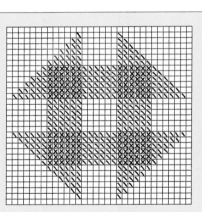

Fig. 3

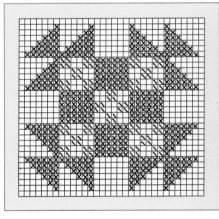

Fig. 4

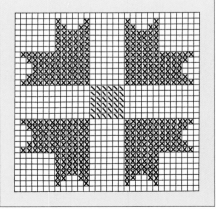

Fig. 5

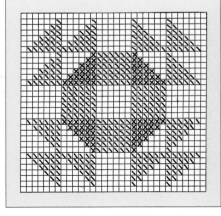

Fig. 6

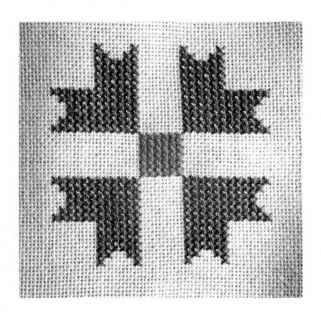

40

PAINTED AND EMBROIDERED COTTAGE

Designed and stitched by Stephanie Simes

Paint your own home or the cottage of your dreams, then
embroider the garden you would love to have.

MATERIALS

30 cm x 40 cm (12 in x 16 in) of linen
Watercolour paints
Fine paintbrush
Black or dark brown fineline
   permanent marker pen
Fine lead pencil
Masking tape
Assorted crewel embroidery needles
Assorted straw needles, including
   size 9
DMC Stranded Cotton: Yellows 676,
   746; Cream 712, Greens 316, 320,
   471, 611, 840, 987, 989, 3346, 3363;
   Browns 645, 844; Pinks 754, 758,
   3689; Blues 209, 327, 792, 793
Minnamurra Threads: Yellow 210,
   Pink 130, Blue 220
Down Under Threads, Waterlilies
   Collection, Olive

Note: The embroidery threads given
here are for this particular garden.

PREPARATION

STEP ONE

Begin by taking a photograph of the
cottage you wish to paint. To ensure
that you have a range of pictures to
choose from, take quite a few views
from different angles.

STEP TWO

For the next step, you will need access
to a photocopier that enlarges, so you
can enlarge the photo to the size you
wish. This may take a couple of
attempts and, with every photocopy,
the picture is slightly distorted. To
rectify this, outline the main features
of the photo in the black or brown
marker pen before every copy. Once
you are satisfied with your photocopy,
outline all the features with the pen
so they are clearly visible.

STEP THREE

Tape the photocopy to a window with
the linen over the top. Trace the main
outlines onto the linen with the pencil.

PAINTING

STEP ONE

Using the watercolours of your choice,
paint the cottage. When loading paint
onto your brush, use a lot of water as
you only want a wash of colour. When
the painting is completed, outline the
features you wish to highlight with
the marker pen.

STEP TWO

Press the linen with a steam iron to set
the paint. From this point on, don't wet
the linen as the paints may still run.

EMBROIDERY

STEP ONE

Photocopy the painted house and use this photocopy to design the garden. The garden does not necessarily have to be true to the picture – this is the perfect opportunity to design the perfect garden for your house.

STEP TWO

Lightly draw in the garden with the pencil. Embroider it in the colours of your choice. The following flowers and stitches relate to the cottage garden pictured here.

STEP THREE

Embroider the fence outline in stem stitch, using one strand of 844.

STEP FOUR

For the standard rose hedge, stitch the stems in chain stitch, using two strands of 840. Work the leaves in a series of lazy daisy stitches using one strand of 3346. The roses are stitched with a size 9 straw needle, using the same method you would use for a bullion rose with the darkest colour in the centre and working to the lighter colour on the outside. Using 758 for the centre colour, work two detached buttonhole stitches, then work a round in 754 with the stitches overlapping each other slightly to give a rose petal effect.

STEP FIVE

Using one strand of the Minnamurra 210, and the size 9 straw needle, stitch a series of bullion roses over the arch. The rose centre has only one bullion stitch with four surrounding stitches. Stitch the leaves in lazy daisy stitch using one strand of Down Under Olive and the stem in stem stitch in the same thread.

STEP SIX

Using one strand of the Minnamurra 130, stitch the hollyhocks, using blanket stitch.

STEP SEVEN

Using one strand of 611, couch the magnolia tree branches and trunk. Stitch the flowers/leaves in blanket stitch in 316. To create the darker colouring on the bottom of the flower, stitch a series of straight stitches in 3689 at the bottom of the flower, coming from the same hole and almost reaching the top of the flower.

STEP EIGHT

Stitch the leaves of the hydrangeas in fishbone stitch, using one strand, alternating 989 with 987. Work the flowers in colonial knots, mixing two strands of Minnamurra 220 with one strand of DMC 793.

STEP NINE

Work the lavender stems in straight stitch and the leaves in fishbone stitch in a mix of one strand of 3363 with one strand of 320. To stitch the flowers, mix one strand of 792 with one strand of 327 and work the flowers in detached buttonhole stitch (Figs. 1-6). On the top of the flower, work two small straight stitches going into the same hole to form a V shape at the top, using one strand of 209.

STEP TEN

Stitch the path in back stitch in one strand of 645.

STEP ELEVEN

For the foxgloves, mix one strand of 712 with one strand of 746 and stitch the flowers in blanket stitch, each time going into the same hole at the top of the flower. Work a series of colonial knots in the same colour under each flower head. Couch the stems with one strand of 471.

STEP TWELVE

Stitch the daisies in two strands of 676 in lazy daisy stitch with colonial knots using two strands of 746 for the centres.

MAKING UP

Do not wash the piece as the paint may run. Carefully press on the wrong side on a fluffy white towel, before having your picture framed.

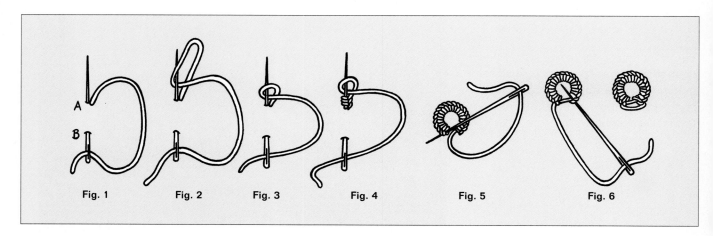

Fig. 1   Fig. 2   Fig. 3   Fig. 4   Fig. 5   Fig. 6

APPLIQUE SCHOOLHOUSE QUILT

Designed and stitched by Stephanie Simes

Recall happy schooldays with this cosy quilt featuring the traditional Schoolhouse block.

MATERIALS

91 cm x 120 cm (36 in x 47 in) piece of doctor flannel

Twelve pieces of fabric, each 22 cm x 28 cm (9 in x 11 in)

2.7 m (3 yd) of backing fabric

Scraps of other fabrics for the stars and trees

85 cm (34 in) of double-sided fusible webbing

Chenille needle, size 24

DMC Perle 8 Cotton, Ecru

Ordinary sewing cotton

Tracing paper

Pencil

PREPARATION

See the templates on the Pull Out Pattern Sheet.

STEP ONE

Wash all the fabrics. Allow them to dry, then press.

STEP TWO

Cut the double-sided fusible webbing into twelve pieces the same size as the fabric pieces. Press the double-sided fusible webbing onto the wrong side of the fabric.

STEP THREE

Trace the house templates and place them on the right side of the fabric pieces. Cut out twelve houses. Save the offcut middle section to use as a placement guide. From the scraps, cut twelve stars, nine small trees, and seven large trees.

STEP FOUR

Sew a line of basting stitches from the top to the bottom of the flannel fabric piece 4 cm (1½ in) from the edge, then another row 25 cm (9⅞ in) away, then another row 4 cm (1½ in) away and so on, until you have eight rows of basting and you are at the end of the fabric. Working from side to side, sew lines of basting 4 cm (1½ in) then 25 cm (9⅞ in) apart as before until you have six rows of basting and you are at the end of the fabric.

MAKING UP

STEP ONE

Place the houses inside the large boxes you have basted. Use the offcut fabric as a placement guide to make them sit evenly. The seam allowance should sit over the edge of the basting lines and will be caught when the sashing is stitched. Peel the paper backing off the double-sided fusible webbing and press the houses into place.

STEP TWO

Cut a piece of the backing fabric exactly the same size as the flannel piece. Pin the backing to the back of the flannel and, using a large zigzag stitch, sew on the backing.

STEP THREE

Cut two strips, each 7 cm x 120 cm (2¾ in x 47 in) from the backing fabric. Turn under 1.5 cm (⅝ in) on both sides so the strips align with the basting, then slipstitch the two centre vertical strips in place. For the outer strips, cut two strips, each 12 cm x 120 cm (4¾ in x 47 in). Attach them in the same way, turning under the raw edge and slipstitching it to the back.

STEP FOUR

For the horizontal sashing, cut three strips, each 7 cm x 91 cm (2¾ in x 36 in). Attach them as before. For the two outer strips, cut two strips, each 12 cm x 105 cm (4¾ in x 41½ in). Attach them in the same way as for the outer vertical strips.

STEP FIVE

Using the Perle Cotton, blanket stitch around the houses. Iron double-sided fusible webbing onto the backs of the stars and trees and appliqué them into place, using the photograph and the placement diagram as a guide. Remove any visible basting threads.

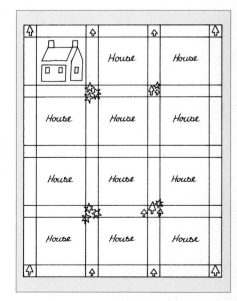

Placement diagram

44

LAVENDER

Designed and stitched by Stephanie Simes

**You can almost smell the heady scent of lavender,
when you gaze at this pretty embroidery.**

MATERIALS

28 cm (11 in) square of Irish linen
DMC Stranded Cotton, one skein
    each: Dark Olive Green 730, Mid-
    grey 927, Grey-green 523, Lilac
    341, Violet 333, Lavender Blue 793
Crewel needle, size 8
Blue water-soluble marker pen
Tracing paper
Masking tape
Black permanent fineline marker pen

PREPARATION

See the embroidery design on page 51.

Trace the design, using the black
marker pen. Tape the tracing to a window with the linen on top. Transfer the
design to the linen, using the blue
marker pen.

EMBROIDERY

STEP ONE

Mix one strand of Mid-grey with three
strands of Grey-green. Use this for the
stems, couched with one strand of
Grey-green.

STEP TWO

Stitch the leaves in fishbone stitch,
using a mix of two strands of Grey-
green with one strand of Mid-grey.

STEP THREE

Stitch the flowers in straight stitch, using
one strand of Lavender Blue. Outline
the flowers in fly stitch, using one
strand of Violet. For the small flowers
on top of the lavender, stitch a colonial
knot, using one strand of Lilac.

STEP FOUR

Complete the border in fly stitch, using
one strand of Dark Olive Green. Using
the same colour, straight stitch the
flower name across the bottom.

MAKING UP

Wash out the blue marker pen with
cool water and a mild soap. While the
linen is still damp, press it on the wrong
side on a fluffy white towel, taking care
not to flatten the embroidery.

Note: Instructions for making the other
three pictures appear on pages 48-51.

POLYGONIUM REYENTRIA

Designed and stitched by Stephanie Simes

A favourite for botanical pictures, this flower also makes a lovely subject for embroidery.

MATERIALS

28 cm (11 in) square of Irish linen
DMC Stranded Cotton, one skein
    each: Hot Pink 961, Rose Pink 962,
    Dark Rose Pink 3687, Mid-green
    3347, Dark Olive Green 730
Crewel needle, size 9
Blue water-soluble marker pen
Tracing paper
Masking tape
Black permanent fineline marker pen

PREPARATION

See the embroidery design on page 51.

Trace the design, using the black marker pen. Tape the tracing to a window with the linen on top. Transfer the design to the linen, using the blue marker pen.

EMBROIDERY

STEP ONE

Stitch the stems in stem stitch, using one strand of Dark Rose Pink.

Stitch the leaves in blanket stitch in two strands of Mid-green. Stitch the vein in straight stitch, using one strand of Dark Rose Pink.

STEP TWO

For the flowers, mix one strand of Hot Pink with one strand of Rose Pink and stitch all the flowers in blanket stitch, commencing at the top of the flower and working down. At the top, all the stitches go into the same hole, fanning out at the other end.

STEP THREE

Complete the border in fly stitch, using one strand of Dark Olive Green. Using the same colour, straight stitch the flower name across the bottom.

MAKING UP

Wash out the blue marker pen with cool water and a mild soap. While the linen is still damp, press it on the wrong side on a fluffy white towel, taking care not to flatten the embroidery.

PRIMULA JAPONICA

Designed and stitched by Stephanie Simes

Elegant leaves topped with a stalk of pink flowers are features of this embroidered picture.

MATERIALS

25 cm x 30 cm (10 in x 12 in) of Irish linen

DMC Stranded Cotton, one skein each: Dark Olive Green 730, Dusty Pink 223, Light Green 3348, Apple Green 471, Light Pink 3689, Yellow 727

Crewel embroidery needle, size 9

Straw needle, size 9

Blue water-soluble marker pen

Tracing paper

Masking tape

Black permanent fineline marker pen

PREPARATION

See the embroidery design on page 51.

Trace the design, using the black marker pen. Tape the tracing to a window with the linen on top. Transfer the design to the linen, using the blue pen.

EMBROIDERY

Note: Use the crewel needle for all the embroidery unless otherwise stated.

STEP ONE

Stitch all the stems in stem stitch, using one strand of Light Green mixed with one strand of Apple Green.

STEP TWO

Stitch the dark leaves in blanket stitch using two strands of Apple Green. Stitch the lighter leaves in blanket stitch in two strands of Light Green.

STEP THREE

Using the straw needle and two strands of Dusty Pink, stitch the buds on the right side of the primula stalk, using bullion stitch.

STEP FOUR

Using one strand of Dusty Pink in the crewel needle, stitch all the dark pink flowers in blanket stitch. Stitch the light pink flowers in blanket stitch, using one strand of 3689. To complete the flower, stitch a colonial knot using two strands of 727.

STEP FIVE

Complete the border in fly stitch, using one strand of Dark Olive Green. Using the same colour, stitch the flower name in straight stitch.

MAKING UP

Wash out the blue marker pen with cold water and a mild soap. Press the linen on the wrong side on a fluffy white towel, taking care not to flatten the embroidery.

PRIMULA VULGARIS

Designed and stitched by Stephanie Simes

Capture the sunshine and bring it indoors with this embroidered primula.

MATERIALS

25 cm x 30 cm (10 in x 12 in) of Irish
    linen
Crewel needle, size 8
DMC Stranded Cotton, one skein
    each: Dark Olive Green 730, Light
    Gold 676, Gold 725, Mid-green
    470, Light Green 3348, Cream 746,
    Brown 420
Blue water-soluble marker pen
Tracing paper
Black permanent fineline marker pen
Masking tape

PREPARATION

See the embroidery design on page 51.

Trace the design from the pattern
sheet, using the black pen. Tape the
tracing to a window and tape the linen
over the top. With the blue marker pen,
trace the design onto the linen.

EMBROIDERY

STEP ONE

Stitch the stem in stem stitch, using one
strand of Mid-green mixed with one
strand of Brown.

STEP TWO

Stitch the leaves in blanket stitch, using
two strands of Mid-green. Stitch the
veins in the leaves in straight stitch,
using one strand of Light Green.

STEP THREE

Stitch the flowers in blanket stitch,
using one strand of Light Gold mixed
with one strand of Gold, leaving the
centre free. Stitch the star-shaped
centre of the flower in straight stitch,
using one strand of Cream. Stitch the
centre of the flowers, using Brown
straight stitch.

STEP FOUR

Stitch the border in fly stitch, using one
strand of Dark Olive Green. Using the
same cotton, straight stitch the flower
name along the bottom.

MAKING UP

Wash out the blue marker pen with
cold water and a mild soap. Press
the linen on the wrong side on a white
fluffy towel, taking care not to flatten
the embroidery.

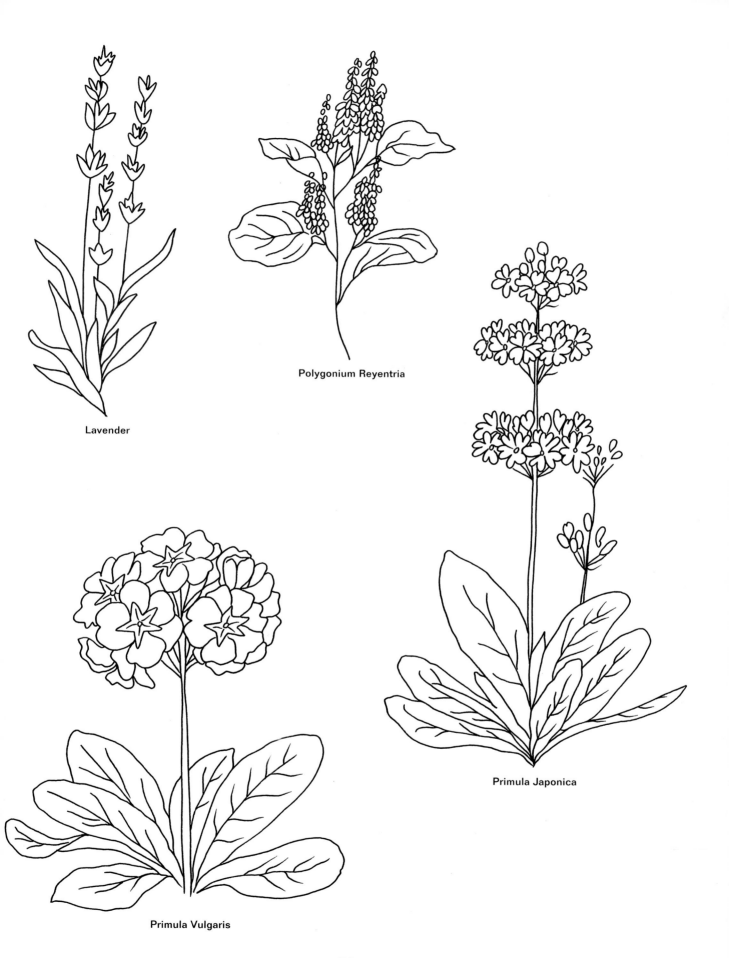

Lavender

Polygonium Reyentria

Primula Japonica

Primula Vulgaris

51

SUNFLOWER QUILT

Designed by Stephanie Simes, stitched by Jenny Taylor and Stephanie Simes

Giant sunflowers appliquéd on flannel adorn this simple quilt.

MATERIALS

135 cm x 140 cm (53 in x 55 in) of doctor flannel

Six large old buttons

25 cm (10 in) of yellow fabric for the flowers

15 cm (6 in) of fabric for the flower centres

30 cm (12 in) of green fabric for the leaves and stems

30 cm (12 in) each of two fabrics for the house

20 cm (8 in) of fabric for the fence

280 cm (110 in) of 115 cm (45 in) wide or 140 cm (55 in) of 140 cm (55 in) wide backing fabric

50 cm (20 in) of double-sided fusible webbing

Blue water-soluble marker pen

Chenille threads: Pecan, Bronze, Bordeaux

Little Wood Fleece Yarn 3 ply Gossamer/Mohair No. 8, Brown/Fawn

Sewing threads to match all the fabrics

Dark-coloured sewing thread for couching

Varying lengths of 115 cm (45 in) wide fabric for the borders

Tracing paper (optional)

Pencil (optional)

PREPARATION

See the templates and embroidery design on the Pull Out Pattern Sheet.

STEP ONE

Wash all the fabrics (except the flannel). Allow them to dry, then press.

STEP TWO

If necessary, piece the backing fabric to achieve the required size. Place the flannel, face down, with the backing fabric, face upwards, on top. Baste the two fabrics together, then machine-stitch with a large zigzag stitch.

ASSEMBLING

STEP ONE

Cut a piece of fusible webbing to fit each piece of fabric, excluding the centres of the flowers. Press the sticky side of the webbing onto the wrong side of the fabric pieces, except for the sunflower and sunflower centre fabrics.

STEP TWO

Trace the patterns. Place them on the right side of the fabric. Cut out the fence, three sunflowers and three flower centres, six leaves, three stems; cut two chimneys and two walls of the house from one fabric, a roof and three windows from the other fabric.

STEP THREE

Turn under the seam allowance on the flower centres and appliqué them into place, then press the fusible webbing onto the wrong side of the flowers.

STEP FOUR

Cut three strips, each 4.5 cm (1³/₄ in) x the length of the green fabric for the stems and leaves. Baste under the 1.5 cm (⁵/₈ in) seam allowance on both sides. Slipstitch the stems into place.

STEP FIVE

On the flannel, measure down 74 cm (29 in) from the top. The bottom of the fence should be roughly along this line. Peel the paper backing off the fusible webbing and press each piece into place, making sure the house and the bottom of the stems tuck under the fence.

EMBROIDERY

STEP ONE

Sew on the large buttons for the flower centres. Using the blue marker pen, draw in the flower petals around the buttons and the motto. Using the chenille threads and the dark sewing thread, couch the flowers, changing colours for each flower. Using one strand of Little Wood Fleece, stitch the motto in stem stitch. Using the matching sewing threads, blanket stitch around all the fabric pieces.

MAKING UP

STEP ONE

Wash out the blue marker pen. Press the work, using a pressing cloth. Join the fabrics for the border to be 15 cm (5⁷/₈ in) wide. With the blue marker pen, mark a line 11 cm (4¹/₄ in) from the edge of the quilt on all four sides. With the right sides facing, sew the side borders along these lines. Trim. Sew the top and bottom borders on in the same way. Turn under the raw edges on the borders and slipstitch them to the back of the quilt.

TIME BEGAN IN A GARDEN

Designed and stitched by Stephanie Simes

Reminiscent of Victorian embroidered sayings, this little
picture has the added charm of appliqué.

MATERIALS

25 cm x 30 cm (10 in x 12 in) of
 cream Dublin linen, 25 count
25 cm x 30 cm (10 in x 12 in) of Pellon
25 cm x 30 cm (10 in x 12 in) of voile
One baby button
Four ceramic buttons, such as a cow,
 a hen and two sunflowers
DMC Stranded Cotton, one skein
 each: Dark Burgundy 3685, Light
 Burgundy 315, Pink 223, Dark
 Yellow 725, Light Yellow 745,
 Purple 208, Ecru, Blue 800, Grey
 646, Dark Green 935, Light Green
 3347, Grey-green 3053, Dark
 Brown 610, Light Brown 612
Tapestry needle, size 24
Quilting needle, size 8
Straw needle, size 8
Three pieces of fabric, each 15 cm
 (6 in) square
Double-sided fusible webbing
Blue water-soluble marker pen
Tracing paper (optional)
Masking tape (optional)
Black permanent fineline marker pen
 (optional)

PREPARATION

See the cross stitch design and the
patterns on page 56.

Find the centre of the linen by folding it
into quarters. Run a basting thread along
the horizontal and vertical folded lines.

CROSS STITCH

Using the tapestry needle and working
with two strands of cotton over two
threads of the linen, stitch the cross
stitch design, following the graph.

APPLIQUE

STEP ONE

Iron the fusible webbing onto the
wrong side of the three pieces of
fabric, making sure the rough side
with the glue on it faces the wrong
side of the fabric.

STEP TWO

Baste the Pellon and the voile to the
back of the linen. Using the pattern
provided, cut out the house and chimneys from one fabric square. From
a different fabric, cut out the roof.
From the third fabric, cut out the door
and windows. Position the house on the
linen with the door lining up with the
centre of the cross-stitched gate.
Pressing with a moderate iron for
approximately fifteen seconds, attach
the house, roof, windows and door
into place.

STEP FOUR

Using one strand of Dark Burgundy
and the quilting needle, blanket stitch
around the house, the roof, chimneys,
windows and door, stitching through
all the layers.

EMBROIDERY

STEP ONE

Using the blue marker pen, draw in
the garden.

STEP TWO

Couch the daisies' stems, using two
strands of Light Green, occasionally
stitching a straight stitch for a leaf.
Along the bottom of the stems, stitch a
few lazy daisy stitches in two strands
of Light Green. Using two strands of
Ecru, stitch a series of lazy daisy
stitches for the flower heads. Fill the
flower centres with colonial knots in
two strands of Dark Yellow.

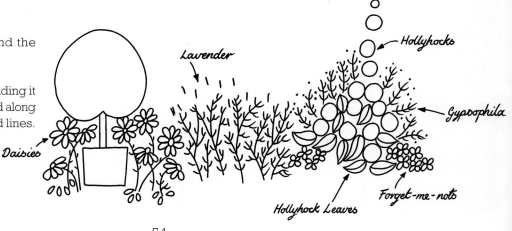

STEP THREE

Stitch the lavender bush in fly stitch in two strands of Grey-green. Stitch the flower heads in bullion stitch, using the straw needle, in a mix of one strand of Purple with one strand of Grey-green.

STEP FOUR

Stitch the leaves of the hollyhocks in fishbone stitch in two strands of Light Green. For the flower heads, use Light Burgundy for the flowers in the centre and Pink for the outside flowers. Work in blanket stitch, starting on the outside of the flower and working your way to the inside. Stitch the top stems and buds in colonial knots, using Light Green and Pink alternately.

STEP FIVE

Stitch the gypsophila, using fly stitch in two strands of Light Green around the hollyhocks. Using two strands of Ecru, stitch colonial knots on the tops of the fly stitch stems.

STEP SIX

For the forget-me-nots, stitch the flower heads in lazy daisy stitch, using two strands of Blue, with a Dark Yellow colonial knot centre.

MAKING UP

STEP ONE

Stitch on the tiny button in the centre of the door. Stitch on the cow button in the garden, the hen above the right-hand chimney and the two sunflowers above the topiary tree.

STEP TWO

Using three strands of the Dark Burgundy, back stitch the motto.

STEP THREE

Wash out any blue marker pen in cold water, then wash the piece, using a mild soap and cold water. Iron carefully around the buttons and embroidery, then frame as desired.

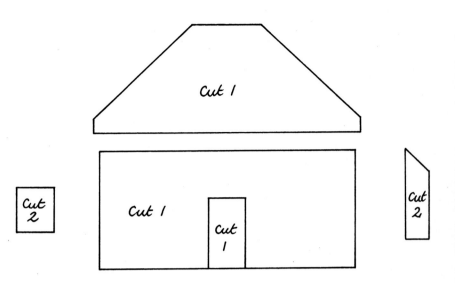

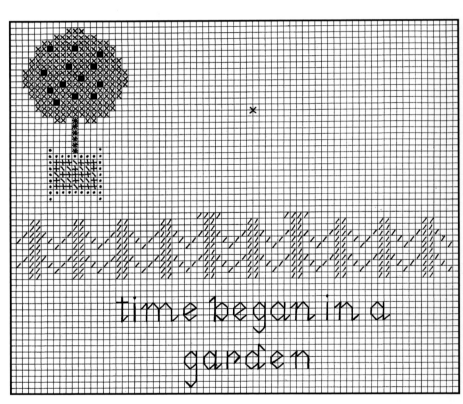

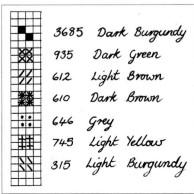

■	3685	Dark Burgundy
✕	935	Dark Green
╱	612	Light Brown
▦	610	Dark Brown
∶	646	Grey
▦	745	Light Yellow
╲	315	Light Burgundy

TEXTURED CUSHION

Designed and stitched by Stephanie Simes

Bring the garden indoors to brighten your favourite chair with this embroidered cushion.

MATERIALS

20 cm x 23 cm (8 in x 9 in) of wool
blanketing
32 cm (12½ in) of fabric for the inner
border
65 cm (26 in) of fabric for the outer
borders and backing
Crewel embroidery wool to match
the inner border fabric
40 cm (16 in) cushion insert
3 mm (³/₁₆ in) wide silk ribbon:
Cream, Purple
Tapestry needles, assorted sizes
DMC Medici Wool: Green 8411,
Yellow 8327
Kirra Yarns 4-ply, Yellow 111
Appleton's Crewel Wool, Rose
Pink 147
Down Under Overdyed Wool, Blue/
Green 14
DMC Stranded Cotton, Green 3012
Little Wood Fleece Yarns: Claret 17,
Green/Brown 6, Dark Green 4
Gossamer/Mohair
Chenille needle, size 24
Tracing paper
Black fineline permanent marker pen
Blue water-soluble marker pen
Ordinary sewing cotton

PREPARATION

See the embroidery design on page 58.

STEP ONE

Trace or photocopy the embroidery
design. Centre the design on the wool
blanketing, then pin and baste around
the wreath shape on the inside and
outside edges. This gives you a guide
for your stitching.

STEP TWO

Remove the paper. Using the blue
marker pen, draw in the flowers. You
may find it easier to cut out each flower
separately from the pattern and trace
around it.

EMBROIDERY

STEP ONE

For the cosmos, using one strand of
Little Wood 17, blanket stitch the
flower, commencing at the outside and
working inwards to create a petal
shape. Using one strand of Little Wood
6, stitch five or six colonial knots for the
centre of the flower. Using the Medici
8327, stitch two or three straight
stitches over the top of each petal.
Stitch the leaves close to the flower so
it gives the impression that the leaf is
coming out from under the flower.
Stitch the leaves in straight stitch, using
one strand of Little Wood 6.

STEP TWO

For the silk daisies, using the Kirra 111,
stitch six or seven colonial knots to
form the centre. Using the Cream
silk ribbon, stitch the petals in lazy
daisy stitch, beginning with a few
stitches at random, then filling in the
gaps. This method will help you to
keep the stitches uniform.

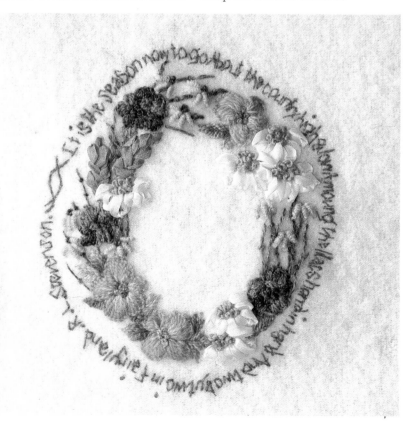

Use this picture to guide your embroidery

STEP THREE

For the cornflowers, using the Down Under Wool, stitch three colonial knots to form the centre, then stitch the petals in blanket stitch. For the bud, use six strands of DMC Stranded Cotton 3012 in blanket stitch. Work the stem in stem stitch.

STEP FOUR

For the yellow daisy stems, using one strand of Little Wood Mohair 4, couch a series of stitches of different lengths. For the daisy petals, work in bullion stitch, using two strands of Medici 8327. Stitch the petals so they droop downwards and make the centre bullion slightly longer than the ones on either side of it.

STEP FIVE

Work the lavender in the Purple silk ribbon, commencing at the top of the flower with one lazy daisy stitch, then work a stitch on either side, working your way down until you have completed the flower. Note how the stitches overlap in the centre. The stem is stitched with two strands of Medici 8411.

STEP SIX

Using one strand of Appleton's 147, stitch the verse in back stitch. 'It is the season now to go about the country high and low. Among the lilacs hand in hand and two by two in fairyland. R.L. Stevenson.'

MAKING UP

STEP ONE

Cut a piece of the inner border fabric, 28 cm x 32 cm (11 in x 12 1/2 in). Centre the wool embroidery on this piece and pin it in place. Using one strand of the matching crewel wool and the crewel needle, blanket stitch all around the embroidered wool, attaching it to the border fabric.

STEP TWO

From the other fabric, cut two strips, each 8 cm x 23 cm (3 1/8 in x 9 in). Stitch these to either side of the block. Cut two more strips 8 cm x 40 cm (3 1/8 in x 15 3/4 in) and sew these to the top and bottom of the block. Press all seams towards the block.

STEP THREE

For the cushion back, cut two pieces of fabric, each 35 cm x 45 cm (13 3/4 in x 17 3/4 in). Hem them both at one short end only. Pin the back to the front with the right sides facing and the back pieces overlapping in the centre. Sew the backs to the front. Trim the seams, turn the cushion cover right side out through the opening and press, taking care not to flatten the embroidery.

Embroidery design

HOT-WATER BOTTLE COVER

Designed and stitched by Jane Toohey

Snuggle into bed on a cold evening with your hot-water bottle tucked
into this pretty cover and you're sure to stay cosy all night.

MATERIALS

28 cm x 80 cm (11 in x 31½ in) of
  wool blanketing
DMC Tapestry Wool, one skein each:
  Blue/black 7339; Pinks 7132, 7151,
  7202, 7204, 7211, 7251; Greens
  7333, 7376, 7377, 7386, 7424, 7426;
  Orange 7124; Yellows 7503, 7504,
  7579; Blues 7314, 7593, 7797, 7799;
  Ecru; Violet 7241, 7262, 7266, 7268;
  Brown 7419; Beige 7521
28 cm x 80 cm (11 in x 31½ in) of
  lining fabric
Doll-making needle
Assorted tapestry needles
Blue water-soluble marker pen
Ordinary sewing cotton to match the
  wool blanketing
80 cm (32 in) of cord or ribbon

Note: For wool embroidery, use a
needle which the wool will comfortably
fit through without causing wear to the
strand. Occasionally, move the position
of the thread in relation to the needle
so the stress is not concentrated at
the same point. This also will reduce
fraying.

  Because wool will not fit through the
eye of a straw needle, a doll-making
needle is used to make an even wrap
on the bullion stitch. The doll-making
needle is similar to a straw or milliner's
needle in that its body and shaft are the
same width, making it easier to pull the
wraps through evenly.

  All the wools used here are tapestry
wools, but some have been stranded.
Use four strands throughout, unless
otherwise instructed.

PREPARATION

See the embroidery design on page 63.

STEP ONE

Fold the wool blanketing in half. Mark
the fold with a line of basting. All the
embroidery will be positioned on one
side (front) of this line.

STEP TWO

Photocopy the design, and cut out each
separate item you are going to stitch,
then trace around it on the front of the
blanketing, using the blue marker pen.

EMBROIDERY

STEP ONE

For the birdhouse, stem stitch the outline in Ecru, then fill in the house in stem
stitch, starting from the top and working
down until the entire area has been
filled. Straight stitch the roof in 7339
until the entire area has been filled in.
Stem stitch the platform and the pole in
two rows of stem stitch in 7339.

STEP TWO

Stem stitch the gate in 7419, filling the
entire shape with stem stitches.

STEP THREE

Stem stitch the path in 7521, creating a
crazy-paving pattern.

STEP FOUR

For the roses over the gate, the centre
is stitched in bullion stitch in two
strands of 7504. The outside wrap is
stitched in bullion stitch in two strands
of 7579. Stitch the leaves in lazy daisy
stitch in two strands of 7426. The stem
is stitched in 7419 stem stitch.

STEP FIVE

Stitch the buds on the topiary tree in fly
stitch with two strands of 7333 around
the buds, stitched in two strands of Ecru.
In the centre, work a fly stitch in two
strands of 7204. Stitch the foliage on the
topiary tree in bullion stitch in two
strands of 7333.

STEP SIX

For the roses on the topiary tree, start
from the centre with three straight
stitches in two strands of 7202. For the
next round, work a series of straight
stitches, following the circle around in
two strands of 7132. For the last round,
work in straight stitch in two strands of
Ecru in the same way. Stitch the stem in
two stem stitch rows of 7333.

STEP SEVEN

Stitch the shaded areas of the hollyhocks in blanket stitch in 7151 and
the rest in blanket stitch in 7211. The
leaves are stitched in small lazy daisy
stitch in 7377.

STEP EIGHT

Stitch the red hot pokers in a series of
bullion stitches in 7124 to form the
flower heads. Work the stems in stem
stitch in 7426.

STEP NINE

Stitch the yellow daisy petals in lazy daisy stitch in 7503. Work French knots in the centre in two strands of 7799.

STEP TEN

Stitch the cream daisy petals in bullion stitch, using two strands of Ecru. Stitch the centre in French knots in two strands of 7503.

STEP ELEVEN

Stitch massed French knots along the path, some in Ecru, some in 7262 and some in 7266. The stems are stitched in straight stitch in 7376.

STEP TWELVE

Stitch the yellow part of the daffodils in 7503 in a series of straight stitches coming to a point at the centre and becoming smaller at the edges. The flower centre is worked in straight stitches in 7124. The stems are stitched in stem stitch in 7426. Work two rows of stem stitch in the same colour for the leaves.

STEP THIRTEEN

The blue flowers are worked in a series of French knots in three strands that are worked in a straight line. The darker colour 7797 at the bottom, next 7593, then 7799 at the top.

STEP FOURTEEN

Stitch the stems of the small orange flowers in stem stitch in two strands of 7376. The flowers are stitched in straight stitch in two strands of 7124.

STEP FIFTEEN

For the forget-me-nots, work the centres in 7503 French knots. The petals are stitched in French knots in 7799.

STEP SIXTEEN

Stitch the pink flowers in lazy daisy stitch in 7251. The foliage is worked in lazy daisy stitch in 7424.

STEP SEVENTEEN

Stitch the foliage of the irises in two rows of stem stitch in 7386, and the stems in one row of the same colour. Stitch the flowers in lazy daisy stitch, placing 7268 on the outside, 7241 on the inside and a French knot in 7503 in the centre.

STEP EIGHTEEN

For the purple flowers on the right side of the path, stitch a series of French knots in 7262, with the leaves in lazy daisy stitch in 7376.

STEP NINETEEN

Stitch the lighter bluebells in buttonhole stitch in 7799. Stitch the darker flowers in buttonhole stitch in 7314 and the leaves in stem stitch in 7426.

STEP TWENTY

Stitch the bird in satin stitch in Ecru. Stitch the beak in straight stitch in one strand of 7124. Stitch a French knot for the eye in one strand of 7799.

MAKING UP

STEP ONE

Stitch two buttonhole stitches by hand in the front of the hot-water bottle cover, approximately 7 cm (2³/₄ in) from the top of the cover.

STEP TWO

Sew the side seams of the embroidered piece and of the lining. Turn the embroidered piece right side out. Place the lining inside the embroidered piece so the wrong sides are facing.

STEP THREE

Turn down 2.5 cm (1 in) on the raw edge of the embroidered piece and 3.5 cm (1³/₈ in) on the raw edge of the lining. Slipstitch the folded edge of the lining to the embroidered piece.

STEP FOUR

Using the ordinary sewing cotton, stitch a casing for the cord or ribbon. Thread the cord or ribbon through the casing.

Embroidery design

HEARTS WALLHANGING

Designed and stitched by Brooke Rozorio

Universal symbols of affection, hearts are the choice for this hand-made gift.

MATERIALS

42 cm x 50 cm (16$^{1}/_{2}$ in x 19$^{1}/_{2}$ in) of homespun

42 cm x 50 cm (16$^{1}/_{2}$ in x 19$^{1}/_{2}$ in) of calico

42 cm x 50 cm (16$^{1}/_{2}$ in x 19$^{1}/_{2}$ in) of wadding

Straw needle, size 8

Quilting needle, size 10

Crewel needle, size 8

Scraps of fabric for the appliqué

Stranded embroidery cottons in Pale Yellow, Yellow, Dark Yellow, Pale Blue, Blue, Pale Pink, Pink, Cream, Pale Green, Green

Quilting thread, Cream

20 cm (8 in) of fabric for the inner border

30 cm (12 in) of fabric for the outer border/binding

Cardboard for templates

Pencil

Tracing paper

Ruler

Water-soluble marker pen

PREPARATION

See the templates and the embroidery designs on pages 66-67.

Note: There are several heart templates of different sizes. Take care to select the correct one for each square.

STEP ONE

Using the ruler and pencil, rule up four 7.5 cm (3 in) squares across and five squares down on the homespun, leaving a 6 mm ($^{1}/_{4}$ in) space between all the squares. Trace the heart templates and cut them out of the cardboard.

STEP TWO

Using template 1, lightly draw in the outline of the heart on squares A, C, F, H, J, M, P, R and U, using the pencil or marker pen.

APPLIQUE

STEP ONE

Using template 1, cut hearts from eight fabrics, adding a 6 mm ($^{1}/_{4}$ in) seam allowance as you cut. The heart in square B has been cut from two fabrics, joined through the centre then cut out, using the same template. Using template 2, cut one heart from one fabric. Using template 3, cut hearts from two fabrics. Using template 4, cut one heart from one fabric and another heart from the joined fabric as before. Using template 5, cut one heart.

STEP TWO

Baste the fabric hearts over the cardboard. Press, then carefully appliqué them by hand, removing the cardboard at the very end, before stitching the remaining edge down. Appliqué all the fabric hearts into place, following the placement guide on page 66.

EMBROIDERY

STEP ONE

For square A, stitch the flowers in lazy daisy stitch in two strands of two different pinks and two different yellows. The leaves are stitched in lazy daisy stitch in two strands of Green. Scatter French knots around the heart, using two strands of two yellows.

STEP TWO

For square C, stitch the forget-me-nots in colonial knots, using two strands of Blue. The centre is worked in colonial knots in three strands of Yellow.

STEP THREE

For square F, work massed colonial knots in three strands of Blue, Yellow and Pink to a width of approximately 6 mm ($^{1}/_{4}$ in) around the heart.

STEP FOUR

For square H, stitch the daffodils in blanket stitch in Darker Yellow with a lazy daisy stitch on either side in Pale Yellow. The stems are in small lazy daisy stitch in Green.

STEP FIVE

For square J, work massed colonial knots in three strands of Blue, Cream and Pale Yellow to a width of approximately 6 mm ($^{1}/_{4}$ in) around the heart.

STEP SIX

For square M, work the wisteria in Blue colonial knots, the stem in Green stem stitch and the leaves in Green lazy daisy stitch.

STEP SEVEN

For square P, work grub roses around the outline of the heart in bullion stitch. The centre of the rose is Dark Yellow, the outer part is Pale Yellow. The leaves are stitched in Green lazy daisy stitch.

STEP EIGHT

For square R, fill the heart with random daisies stitched in lazy daisy stitch in Pale Yellow, Dark Yellow and Pink; forget-me-nots in Blue colonial knots with a Yellow colonial knot centre. The leaves are worked in Green lazy daisy stitch. Fill the gaps with colonial knots in mixed colours.

STEP NINE

For square U, divide the heart into a 12 mm (½ in) squared grid with running stitch in two strands of Blue. Stitch around the heart in the same way. Sew grub roses in two shades of pink at the intersections of the grid.

MAKING UP

STEP ONE

Cut the inner border fabric into 2.5 cm (1 in) wide strips. Sew the side borders on first, then the top and, bottom borders.

STEP TWO

Cut the outer border/binding fabric into 6 cm (2½ in) wide strips. Sew the side borders on first, then the top and bottom borders.

STEP THREE

Place the calico backing with the wadding on top and the completed top on top of that. Baste the three layers together. Quilt two rows of stitching 6 mm (¼ in) apart between the squares and around the outside of the quilt.

STEP FOUR

Turn 3 cm (1¼ in) of the outer border to the wrong side of the quilt. Turn under the raw edge and slipstitch the folded edge to the back of the quilt. Stitch two tabs at the back from which to hang the quilt.

Placement Guide

Square A

Square C

Square F and J

Square H

Square M

Square P

Square R

Square U

67

CANDLEWICKING QUILT

Designed and stitched by Stephanie Simes

Classic cream, this superb quilt is sure to become a treasured heirloom.

MATERIALS

6 m (6½ yd) of 115 cm (45 in) wide homespun seeded fabric for the blocks and ruching

Sufficient fabric for the borders and backing (see the note below)

Sufficient thin wadding (see the note below)

Sufficient satin blanket binding

20 m (22 yd) of edging braid

Chenille needles, assorted sizes

Crewel needles, assorted sizes

Beeswax

Blue water-soluble marker pen

30 cm (12 in) embroidery hoop

DMC Stranded Cotton, Ecru

DMC Broder Cotton No. 16, Ecru

DMC Perle Cotton Nos 3, 5, 8, 12, Ecru

Crown Perle Rayon, Ecru

DMC Flower Thread, Ecru

Ordinary sewing cotton

Tracing paper

Black fineline permanent marker pen

Pencil

Masking tape

Cotton tape

Note: The amount of fabric given here makes the twelve blocks with the ruching between. You will need to measure your bed and add borders appropriate to that particular bed and allow enough fabric for the backing, and enough wadding.

PREPARATION

See the embroidery designs on the Pull Out Pattern Sheet.

STEP ONE

Preshrink all the fabric by washing it in hot water. Press the fabric while it is slightly damp.

STEP TWO

Cut twelve 40 cm (16 in) squares from the homespun or 39.5 cm (15½ in) if you are using a precut quilter's block. From the remaining fabric, cut three strips 280 cm (112 in) long and 10 cm (4 in) wide. Cut eight strips 80 cm (32 in) long and 10 cm (4 in) wide.

STEP THREE

To transfer the embroidery designs, trace each design from the pattern sheet, using the black marker pen. Tape the tracing to a window. Centre the fabric square over the tracing and trace the design onto the fabric, using the blue marker pen. There are six designs, all repeated once and stitched in different cottons to give each one a slightly different look.

1a	4a	2a
3	6	5a
4b	2b	1b
5b	3	6

Placement diagram

EMBROIDERY

Bind the hoop with the tape to prevent it leaving marks on the fabric, then place each square in turn in the hoop. Work the embroidery in the stitches and threads indicated on the design, using the appropriate needles for the thread being used. Do not be concerned if the knots are flattened as you move the fabric around in the hoop. They will return after washing.

STEP ONE

For block 1a, using a chenille needle and six strands of DMC Stranded Cotton that has been run through beeswax, stitch the four centre leaves in fishbone stitch. Using one strand of Perle 8 Cotton, stem stitch around the leaf. Using Broder Cotton, couch the marked grid. With Perle 5 Cotton, stitch the border in herringbone stitch.

STEP TWO

For block 1b, work in the same way as for 1a, except that the stem stitch outline is worked in Perle 5 Cotton, the couching is worked in the DMC Flower Thread and the herringbone is worked in Perle 3 Cotton.

STEP THREE

For block 2a, stitch all the dots in colonial knots, using Perle 5 Cotton. Couch the grid on the hearts with the Crown Perle Rayon, stem stitching around the hearts in the same thread.

STEP FOUR

For block 2b, work in the same way as for 2a, except that the colonial knots are stitched in six strands of the stranded cotton and the hearts are couched and outlined in the Broder Cotton.

STEP FIVE

For block 3, stitch the outline of the hearts in colonial knots using Perle 3 Cotton. Stitch the grid boxes using the Perle 12 Cotton, stitching the lines as marked and making sure you catch all the stitches with a catching thread. The dots in the centre box are colonial knots, stitched in two strands of Perle 12 Cotton. The squares are stitched in back stitch in one strand of Perle 12 Cotton.

STEP SIX

For block 4a, stitch the dots in colonial knots, using Perle 3 Cotton. Using the Crown Perle Rayon, stitch the pattern in the leaf in running stitch; do not stitch the centre line. Stitch the outline of the leaf in stem stitch. Stitch the scroll designs in stem stitch in the Broder Cotton.

STEP SEVEN

For block 4b, stitch the dots in colonial knots using the Perle 3 Cotton. Stitch the lines inside the leaf and the centre line in running stitch, using the Crown Perle Rayon. Stem stitch the outside of the leaf in Crown Perle Rayon. Work all the rest of the stitching in running stitch, using the Crown Perle Rayon.

STEP EIGHT

For block 5a, stitch all the dots in colonial knots, using three strands of Broder Cotton. Do not stitch the tulips in the centre.

STEP NINE

For block 5b, stitch all the dots in colonial knots, using six strands of stranded cotton. Stitch the tulip design in the centre, using six strands of stranded cotton and fishbone stitch. Stitch every second tulip centre in fly stitch instead of fishbone stitch, still using the stranded cotton.

STEP TEN

For block 6, stitch all the dots in colonial knots, using Perle 3 Cotton. Stitch the rest of the design in running stitch, using the Crown Perle Rayon.

MAKING UP

STEP ONE

Cut sixteen 40 cm (16 in) lengths of the braid. Stitch the braid to the right side of each block 6 mm (1/4 in) from the side edges, with the finished side facing the design. Repeat this for all the blocks.

STEP TWO

On the 80 cm (32 in) strips of homespun, sew two rows of gathering thread down each side, using the ordinary sewing thread. Gather up each strip to fit one side of the blocks. With the right sides facing, pin a gathered strip to one side of a block. Turn the block over so the back of the design faces you, and stitch the strip and the block together along the stitching line of the braid. Turn to the right side. Repeat this procedure until you have joined three blocks together with the ruched sashing in between. Make four rows of blocks and sashing.

STEP THREE

Next, gather the long strips of homespun and attach the braid in the same way as before. Join the four rows to form the centre of the quilt. Cut and stitch braid around all the edges of the pieced centre.

STEP FOUR

Cut strips of homespun of the desired widths for the borders. Attach the borders to the four sides of the quilt.

STEP FIVE

Measure the quilt with the borders attached and cut the backing 10 cm (4 in) larger all around. Place the backing face down on a large table or the floor. Centre the wadding on top and then the quilt top on top of that. Baste the three layers together until the quilt is very firm, then quilt as desired. This quilt has been stipple-quilted around the blocks and large borders with a small heart design for the outside of the blocks. The quilting was done with a quilting machine. You can quilt with any design you choose.

STEP SIX

When the quilting is completed, bind all the quilt edges with the blanket binding.

CUSHIONS

To make any of these quilt blocks into cushions, cut and stitch the designs as instructed. Attach braid around the edges of the block as for the quilt. Cut a strip of fabric 20 cm x 230 cm (8 in x 90 in). Join the ends to form a loop. Press the loop over double with the wrong sides facing. Sew two rows of gathering stitches 1.5 cm (5/8 in) from the raw edge and gather it up to fit the block. Pin the ruffle around the block, adjusting the gathering to make it even and placing a little extra fullness at the corners. Stitch the ruffle in place. Cut a 40 cm (16 in) square of fabric for the back. Sew the front to the back with the right sides facing, leaving an opening on one side, trim the seams and turn the cover right side out. You can either slipstitch the opening closed or insert a zipper.

CHATELAINE

Designed and stitched by Stephanie Simes

An essential tool for stitchers in the past, today's chatelaine is an object of beauty.

MATERIALS

50 cm (20 in) of grosgrain moiré taffeta
Embroidery scissors
3.6 m (4 yd) of cream edging braid
1 m (1¹/₈ yd) of cream and gold twisted cord
4 m (5 yd) of narrow cream cord
4 m of 7 mm (⁵/₁₆ in) wide silk ribbon, Cream
Tapestry needle, size 24
Crewel needle, size 7
Two gold bow charms
25 cm (10 in) of wadding
Small amount of polyester fibre fill
Gold/brass clasp
Small amount of wool blanketing or felt for the needlecase
Blue water-soluble marker pen
Rajmahal Silks: Greens 44, 311, 421, 742, 745
Madeira Metallic Thread, Gold 9803-3004
Kreinik Japan Gold #5 and 002J
Small gold ring
Tracing paper
Black fineline permanent marker pen

PREPARATION

See the pattern and the embroidery design on the Pull Out Pattern Sheet.

STEP ONE

Cut out the pattern pieces from the moiré fabric as directed, cutting four pockets, four backs, four needlecases and one pincushion. From the wadding, cut two pockets and two backs.

STEP TWO

Trace the embroidery design, using the black marker pen. Transfer the embroidery design onto two of the pockets. To do this, tape the tracing to a window with the pocket fabric over the top. Trace the design onto the fabric, using the blue marker pen.

STEP THREE

Baste the wadding to the back of the two pocket pieces.

EMBROIDERY

Note: Use crewel needles for the embroidery, unless stated otherwise.

STEP ONE

Stitch the stem in stem stitch, using one strand of Rajmahal 311, one strand of 421 and one strand of 44 together. Using the same thread combination, stitch the top leaf in fishbone stitch. Stitch the middle leaf in three strands of Rajmahal 421 and the bottom leaf in three strands of Rajmahal 311.

STEP TWO

Outline the leaves, using the Madeira Metallic Thread couched with the Kreinik 002J thread.

STEP THREE

Stitch the centre of the flower in satin stitch, using the Rajmahal 44 thread. Stitch the petals in satin stitch, using the tapestry needle and silk ribbon to form a heart shape.

Note: The designs on the two pockets are exactly the same, but the colouring of the leaves has been altered.

STEP FOUR

Stitch the swirl on the bottom right-hand side in stem stitch, using one strand of the Kreinik #5. Work all the gold stitching around the flower petals, the flower centre and colonial knots in the same thread.

STEP FIVE

Using the Kreinik 002J thread, stipple-quilt the entire area around the design, starting from the centre and working towards the edges.

STEP SIX

After all the embroidery is completed, wash out the blue marker pen, before assembling the chatelaine, making sure all the fabric is quite dry.

MAKING UP

STEP ONE

Stitch a strip of the edging braid across the top of both pockets. Stitch each pocket to one back piece, stitching around the curved edge.

STEP TWO

Baste the backs together in pairs with the wrong sides facing and the wadding sandwiched in between.

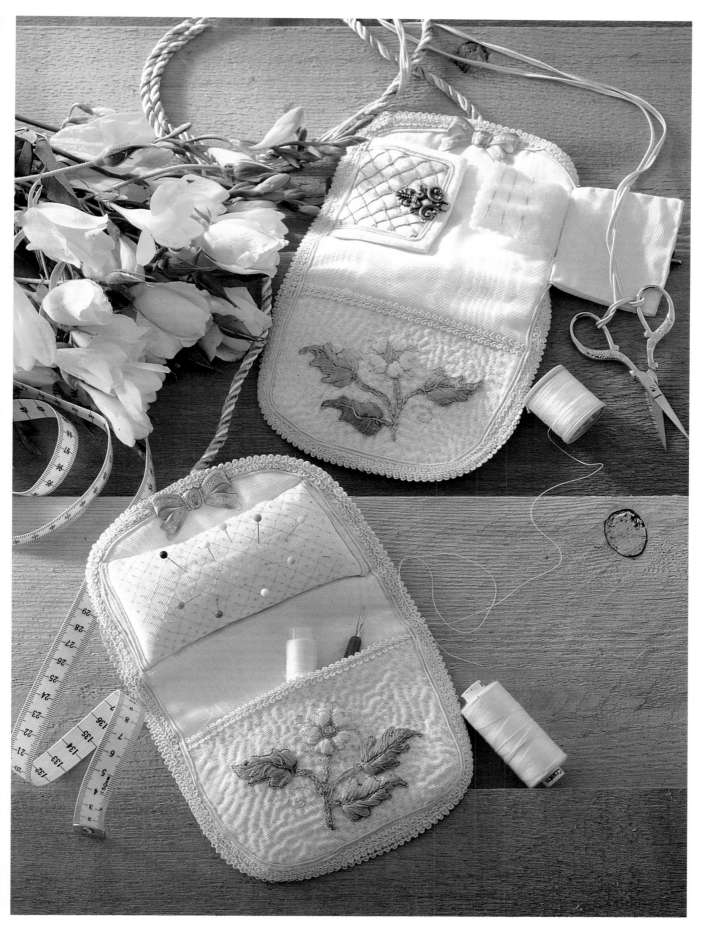

STEP THREE

Transfer the grid design onto the centre 7.5 cm (3 in) of the pincushion piece. Using the Kreinik 002J Gold thread, couch the grid lines, then work colonial knots in the spaces. When the embroidery is completed, fold the piece with the right sides together. Stitch the long sides to form a loop. Fold the loop so the seam falls at the centre back and the embroidery is on top. Stitch one end closed. Turn the pincushion to the right side. Stuff the pincushion to the required depth with the fibre fill, then stitch the other end closed. Stitch the ends of the pincushion to the back piece as shown.

STEP FOUR

Transfer the grid design onto two needlecase pieces. Couch the Madeira Metallic Thread along the lines, using the Kreinik 002J to couch. Place the needlecase pieces together in pairs, with the right sides facing. Stitch around three sides. Turn the piece to the right side. Machine-sew narrow cream cord around the couching. Cut four pieces of blanketing or felt and pin these to the back of the needlecase along the open edge. Sew the sides of the needlecase to opposite sides of the other back piece. Sew on the gold/brass clasp, making sure the two sides of the clasp meet.

STEP FIVE

Sew the edging braid around the front and back of both pockets, beginning and ending at the top. Stitch a row of narrow cream cord inside the edging braid. Neaten the joins of the braid and cord and sew a gold bow charm over the join.

STEP SIX

Knot the gold and cream twisted cord at each end. Attach the cord to the back of each pocket at the top, using fine stitches that are not visible. Halfway along the cord, attach the gold ring, then, using the remaining narrow cream cord, attach the embroidery scissors to the ring.

WOOL BLANKET WITH BOWS

Designed and stitched by Stephanie Simes

Graceful bows and spring flowers decorate this pretty blanket, combining with the checked border for a country look.

Finished size: 110 cm x 160 cm (43½ in x 63 in)

MATERIALS

110 cm x 160 cm (43½ in x 63 in) of wool blanketing or any size that will comfortably fit the pattern
DMC Tapestry Wool: Blues 7287, 7593, 7800
DMC Stranded Cotton, Yellow 744
Appleton's Crewel Wool: Dusty Pink 147, Rose Pink 143, Dull Rose Pink 142, Lavender 604, Yellow 842
Little Wood Variegated Fleece Yarns, Green/Brown no. 6
3 mm (³⁄₁₆ in) wide silk ribbon, Cream
Tapestry needles, assorted sizes 18-24
Tracing paper
Black fineline permanent marker pen
Ordinary sewing cotton (for basting) in the same shade as DMC Tapestry Wool 7287
Blue water-soluble marker pen
Scraps of fabric, Klostern, Aida and/or linen for the backing (optional)
Stranded cotton for embroidering some of the backing squares (optional)
2 m (2¼ yd) of checked cotton fabric for the borders
4.6 m (5 yd) of narrow braid

PREPARATION

See the embroidery design on the Pull Out Pattern Sheet.

Note: The embroidery design given is one-quarter of the complete design. Repeat the design four times to make the complete wreath.

STEP ONE

Photocopy the design four times. Tape the sections together, cut around the inside and outside of the design to give the shape of the wreath. Pin this to the centre of the wool blanketing. To make sure the design is centred accurately, measure from the edge of the wreath to the fabric edge on all sides, making sure they are equal. Baste around the inside and outside of the paper pattern, then remove the pattern.

STEP TWO

To transfer the bows, trace and cut out four bows and pin them to the wreath, close to the inside edge, making sure they are evenly spaced. Baste around the bows with the sewing cotton, then remove the paper. You will be left with the shape of the bows to embroider.

STEP THREE

To transfer all the other flowers, trace the design onto tracing paper. Use this as a guide for placement, stitching the flowers freehand.

EMBROIDERY

STEP ONE

Stitch the bows in satin stitch, using DMC Tapestry Wool 7287. Make sure you change the direction of the wool, when the bow 'changes direction'. This gives an impression of movement.

STEP TWO

For the wool roses, the centre is stitched with two strands of Appleton's Crewel Wool 147, using six straight stitches approximately 15 mm (⅝ in) long to form a square (Fig. 1). Next, stitch directly back over the top of these stitches to form a padded square. With two strands of Appleton's Crewel Wool 143, stitch four straight stitches across the bottom third of the square (Fig. 2). The bottom of the square should no longer be visible. Turn your work clockwise until the stitches just stitched are on the left-hand side of the square, then stitch another four stitches across the bottom of the square as before (Fig. 3). Repeat this twice more until all the edges of the square are covered (Fig. 4).

STEP THREE

Using two strands of Appleton's Crewel Wool 142 and commencing in the middle of the bottom of the square, stitch two straight stitches across to the middle of the right-hand side of the square (Fig. 5). Bring the needle up at the right-hand corner of the square. Turn your work clockwise so the next two stitches you will do will be stitched from that corner to the corner directly above (Fig. 6). Bring the needle up at the centre of the right-hand side of the

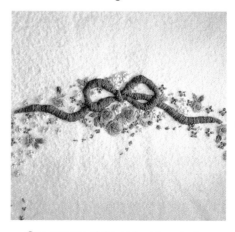

One-quarter of the embroidery design

square and work two stitches across to the centre of the top of the square. Bring the needle up at the corner, turn the work and repeat this process: centre to centre, corner to corner, until the first stitch meets the last stitch. Now you have one more lot of two and a half stitches to go. Stitch two stitches from corner to corner, then tuck the last half-stitch into the centre of the right-hand side of the rose. Work three of these roses on top of each of the bows. Work the smaller roses in the same way, but omit the four rounds of straight stitch across the bottom of the square.

STEP FOUR

Stitch the leaves in fishbone stitch, using one strand of Little Wood Fleece.

STEP FIVE

Stitch the lavender in two strands of Appleton's Crewel Wool 604. Using the water-soluble marker pen, draw in the curved lines for the lavender. Starting at the bottom, stitch one straight stitch,

then working from side to side, stitch another straight stitch on either side of the first one and slightly shorter but going into the same hole at the bottom. Stitch two more stitches, one either side of the others, making these smaller again. Complete the stem of lavender, reducing the number of stitches by one each time, until there is only one remaining.

STEP SIX

Using two strands of Appleton's 842, stitch five or six colonial knots to form a small centre for the daisies. Using a short length of the silk ribbon, work a series of straight stitches to form the daisy petals.

STEP SEVEN

Stitch the forget-me-nots using DMC Tapestry Wool 7593 and 7800 alternately, working small straight stitches and going over the same stitch and into the same hole twice. Dot them in the wreath at random. The centre is a colonial knot, stitched in six strands of DMC Stranded Cotton 744.

MAKING UP

STEP ONE

Remove the basting threads. This blanket has a scrap patchwork back. Cut a series of squares in the desired size. If you wish, cut some of these squares from Klostern, Aida or linen and cross stitch these squares or appliqué designs on them. Join the squares until you reach the desired size. Baste the wool piece and the patchwork piece together with the wrong sides facing.

STEP TWO

Cut four 28 cm (11 in) wide border strips. Sew the top and bottom strips to the patchwork side of the blanket with the right sides facing. Sew on the side borders in the same way. Bring the border onto the front of the blanket, mitring the corners. Turn under the raw edge and slipstitch the edges onto the blanket. Sew on the braid over the edge of the border.

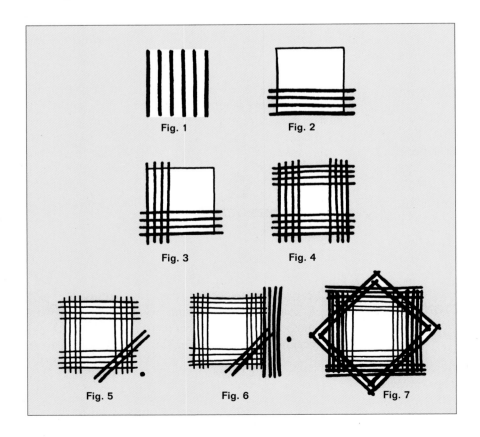

COUNTRY GARDEN COLLAGE

Designed and made by Annette Phelps

The warmth of terracotta, combined with a posy of dried flowers is very appealing. Attached to weathered board, it has a truly rustic feel.

MATERIALS

Fence post framed board
   approximately 45 cm x 50 cm
   (18 in x 20 in)
Two terracotta half-pots, 9 cm
   (3½ in) diameter
Dry foam
Dried flowers, such as larkspur,
   safflower, lavender, daisy
Dried bud green foliage
Sphagnum moss
Mushrooms
Raffia
Glue gun
Lichen (optional)

ASSEMBLING

STEP ONE

Cut the foam to fit the half-pots, then glue the pots and foam to the board.

STEP TWO

Working on the right-hand pot first, place the lavender in the middle of the foam to form a stack with varying heights. Place moss around the base of the lavender to cover the foam.

STEP THREE

Make a small bow from the raffia and glue it at the base of the lavender.

STEP FOUR

Glue the mushrooms at the side of the pot.

STEP FIVE

For the left-hand pot, place the dried bud green foliage at the back of the pot, graduating to either side of the pot in an A-shape. Place the safflower in between. Fill in with daisy and larkspur, making sure to use small pieces so as not to make the arrangements too heavy looking.

STEP SIX

Tie another raffia bow and glue it to the front of the pot. For an extra rustic effect, glue lichen to the frame.

STITCH GUIDE

FISHBONE STITCH

Work one straight stitch at the end, extending it slightly over the outline. Begin working stitches alternately to the left and right of the centre, overlapping them in the centre as shown.

FRENCH KNOT

Bring the needle up through the fabric where you wish the knot to sit. Wind the thread once around the needle. Gently pulling the thread tight, reinsert the needle at the point of exit and pull the thread through. Bring the needle up through the fabric ready for the next French knot.

BULLION STITCH

Bullion stitches are used either on their own, or in groups to create roses. To make a bullion stitch, bring the needle through at **a** then take a stitch to **b**, bringing the needle back out at **a** without pulling the needle right through. Wrap the thread around the needle, covering the length from **a** to **b**. Pull the needle through and slide the wraps off the needle, easing them down until they are lying on the fabric. Reinsert the needle at **b** to secure the bullion.

FLY STITCH

Fly stitch is frequently used for leaves and is worked as an open lazy daisy stitch in ribbon, cotton or wool. Begin by bringing the needle through from the back just to the left of where you wish to place the stitch. Reinsert the needle one stitch length away to the right and take a small stitch back to the centre, keeping the point of the needle over the ribbon, cotton or wool. Pull the needle through and secure the stitch with a small vertical stitch.

COLONIAL KNOT

Bring the thread from the back of the work at **a**. Pass the needle under the thread. Turn the needle to the left and the thread will twist over the needle as though you are making a figure eight with the thread around the needle. Pull the thread firmly to the base of the needle, then take the needle through to the back of the work at **b**.

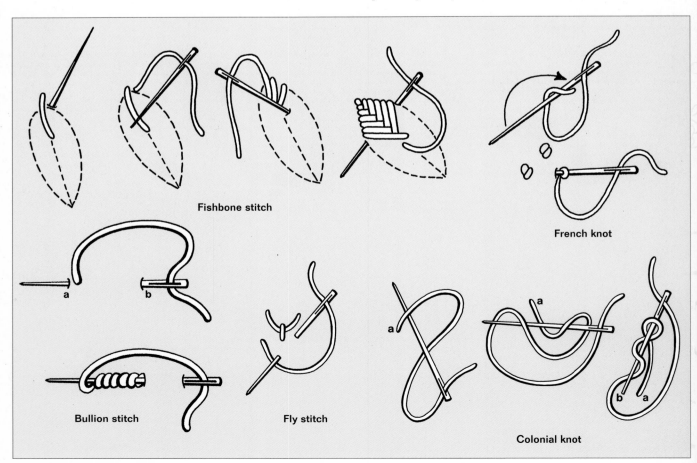

Fishbone stitch

French knot

Bullion stitch

Fly stitch

Colonial knot